To Amy Schlein, Anab Jafri, Bridget Arsenault,
Catherine McCauley, Chris Mallinos, Corinne Impey,
Drew Davidson, Heather Farragher, Henry Claflin, Rebecca
McAllister, Sapna Goel and TJ Arch. Thank you for the countless
hours you've put in helping to turn an idea into an educational
resource, each and every week.

Contents

Foreword
By Archbishop Desmond Tutu

I think I was about nine-years-old when I found a tattered copy of *Ebony* magazine that contained an article about Jackie Robinson.

He was an African-American baseball player who broke into the major leagues to play for the Brooklyn Dodgers. For me, a small boy sitting in a South African ghetto township in the midst of apartheid, his heroic struggle was a great influence.

Here was a man who had overcome enormous adversity and suffered tremendous abuse for simply following his dreams. His example made me feel several inches taller. Jackie Robinson left the impression that we should do what we can. In the end, by standing up to that bully, you win a little victory for righteousness and you give others the example to stand up for truth.

This isn't the kind of thing that often makes banner headlines. But, it does make a difference. It made a difference to me. That's what I try to remember when reading through the other headlines.

You would not be a normal person if you were not sometimes, somewhat depressed by the news reports we get today. It's news of war, conflict, violence, disease, poverty. You would be very odd if sometimes you didn't feel shocked.

But is that in fact the whole picture? We have seen the Berlin Wall collapse. We have seen the shackles that bound people for so long, as in South Africa, fall from their wrists and ankles. We have seen a small, little woman dispense compassion and caring and love in Calcutta.

These stand as proof of the fact that this is, in fact, a moral universe. It's evidence that injustice can never have the last word.

I remember coming to North America in the '80s, at a time when my own country was in turmoil. I was especially exhilarated by young people. On university and college campuses, I met with students who ought to have been worried about their grades. Instead, by reading about our struggle, they found inspiration to demonstrate and worry about people thousands of miles away.

Today, you belong in this long line of fantastic young people. Our lives are not atomistic. Instead, we are connected with those who have gone before as we will be connected with those who come after.

When we look at the state of the world, we sometimes wonder whether God has any plan at all. God sees our inhumanity to one another. But He also sees you as you help and you help and you help, and God smiles.

This is because evil is not the norm. Injustice, poverty and war are not the norm. They are aberrations.

The norm is goodness. The norm is compassion. The norm is gentleness. And you and I are created for goodness.

As you read through this compilation, remember that you wouldn't be normal if you didn't feel somewhat depressed. But, as you read, remember that there are incredible things, beautiful things that happen in the world. One is the fact that you, me and many other people are appalled by violations of human rights.

In Southern Africa, we have a concept called *Ubuntu* – which is that you can't exist as a human being in isolation. You can't be human all by yourself. What you do, what I do, affects the whole world.

When you do good, it spreads that goodness. Since that day in the South African ghetto when I found that tattered magazine, I have been blessed more each day with the happiness that springs from this truth.

May 2010

Introduction

It was early in Craig's trip to South Asia when he visited one of the largest slums in Bangladesh.

There were no schools, no hospitals, no sanitation. Most of the kids worked in factories under dangerous conditions, making miniscule wages to help support their impoverished families. The conditions were absolutely heartbreaking.

Seeing kids his age and younger working in such conditions was devastating for Craig. It seemed so unfair that his life in Canada could be so different than here in Bangladesh. Through tears that were half sadness, half anger, he asked one aid worker what he could do to help.

"Go home," the young man stated simply. "Be a witness. Tell others what you saw and ask them if they think it's fair."

It's impossible to count the number of times we've heard this sentiment expressed by ordinary individuals we've met in our travels. In all corners of the globe, storytelling is a longstanding tradition with significance that's lost on no one. It's vital to preserving culture. It speaks of moments of pride. It speaks of moments of injustice. It offers an opportunity to learn. Most importantly, it inspires us to create change for the future.

In the years since, we've tried to pass on these stories to anyone who will listen. We've done our best to describe the unbearable conditions under which children are forced to work so that others can understand the extent of the problem. At the same time, we've spoken of the joy and the excitement that appears on a child's face as they write solutions to math equations on a chalkboard in a newly built classroom.

Stories that speak of injustice and others that speak of hope are equally important. Through both, we've tried to challenge others to look within themselves and ask how they can be part of making a difference.

In 2006, we were approached to write a weekly column called Global Voices. The goal was to cast light on the untold stories of people and issues from around the world. Our hope was that it would help spark conversations about current affairs across the country.

We were humbled to be included in the newspapers that we read growing up. At the same time we recognized the opportunity before us. A speech could reach a few hundred, maybe even a few thousand at a time. A weekly column could present these stories to countless more, every single week.

So often, when you open the newspaper, the commentary and quotations come from a select group of individuals. They are usually those in positions of power, not those who are affected by their words. Our mission became to broaden that voice, to make it truly global. We wanted to offer others the chance to experience the world through the stories of those whose voices are often suppressed – those who often don't get a chance to speak out.

These voices included John Mafinder, a 15-year-old former child soldier we met in Sierra Leone. This young man asked the world if it was fair that his childhood was taken away when he was handed an AK-47 and forced to raid a village.

It was also 12-year-old Surmaal from the village of Lai, India who asked directly for a greater focus on water in his country. He couldn't go to school as he spent his day traversing two hills to retrieve the vital resource from the closest well in the parched region.

The column then became a space for a group of university students in Port-au-Prince to sing their country's national anthem while hoisting the Haitian flag in front of the collapsed Presidential Palace. Just days after an earthquake devastated their country, their solidarity, faith and determination that their country would persevere through this crisis was something we felt the entire world should hear.

Over the last four years, we have tried to offer these stories as a means to encourage conversation and motivate action. The column currently appears weekly in the *Toronto Star*, *Vancouver Sun* and the *Huffington Post*. Its accompanying curriculum is distributed to nearly 5,000 educators who use them with students, in-class. The program has also expanded to offer students the chance to put their writing skills to action through the Junior Journalists program, a group of talented young reporters whose articles appear alongside Global Voices on the *Toronto Star's* website.

Now, we hope this compilation will serve as an additional means to present these stories and inspire you the way each person featured has inspired us.

We understand that flicking through headlines can get depressing. In fact, we should probably point out that there was a time where we stopped reading the newspaper altogether. It was part of an ill-conceived effort to start our day on a brighter note.

It was quickly shot down by a conversation with a man we've had the honour of calling a mentor – Archbishop Desmond Tutu. The Nobel Peace Prize winner is best known for opposing apartheid in South Africa and as a vocal supporter of human rights worldwide. So, when he said, "You're looking at this in completely the wrong way," we listened.

What we saw as depressing, he saw as "God's To-Do List," delivered right to his front door every morning. We don't think you have to be a person of any particular faith to appreciate these words. As the Archbishop explained, he started his morning by taking the newspaper and putting it flat on the kitchen table. Together with his kids and grandkids, they would read it like a menu.

If you're passionate about local issues, it's the first couple pages. If you want to make a difference nationally, go midway through. If your passion is changing the world, it's always at the end. Whatever your issue, it's conveniently divided out, every single day – a call to action right on your doorstep.

We've tried to do the same with this compilation. Each section is divided by issue and contains some of the stories that have been most inspiring to us. We hope that by reading this collection with your friends, family or classmates, it inspires discussion and helps you find your passion.

Most of all, we hope you find inspiration by hearing these stories from around the world. We hope you will begin to see these columns as a message from a neighbour, a friend, a voice in your global community.

Be The Change,

Craig and Marc Kielburger
April 2010

1
Children & Education

It was a headline in the newspaper about Iqbal Masih that started Free The Children back in 1995. It's no coincidence we started this compilation in the same vein.

One April morning, Craig reached for the comics and found a headline reading, "Battled child labor, boy, 12, murdered." That article drove Craig to take action. Since then, the stories we've heard from other kids around the world have served as further inspiration for the work we do.

Behind each of these stories, we've found a desire for education. We believe it is the cornerstone to development. Former United Nations Secretary General Kofi Annan once said, "Education is peace-building by another name." In a more practical sense, we've seen with just a few years of primary education, girls get married later and learn the steps they need to take to prevent HIV/AIDS.

Education empowers young people to lift themselves out of poverty and provide a better life for their families. Despite knowing this, there are still an estimated 121 million kids of primary school age who are denied the opportunity to attend school and 218 million children working as child labourers under extremely hazardous conditions.

While the statistics speak for themselves, we think it's more important to let the children do the talking.

The voice might come from a group of street children in India who run their own bank, financing loans to help lift each other out of poverty. It might be that of a young girl trapped in a cycle of poverty and violence in the midst of Mexico's deadly drug war. While their stories are unique, each speaks to the challenges that fall on their young shoulders in a way that statistics simply can't.

In 2009, we marked 20 years since the signing of the United Nations Convention on the Rights of the Child. There was so much hope with the signing of this document. It was the first to enshrine the civil, cultural, economic, political and social rights of children. It remains the most widely-ratified convention in history.

Most of the young people mentioned in this section aren't old enough to remember the signing of this document. Sadly, they haven't seen the benefits of it either. Few countries have lived up to their promise to protect children – Canada is one of them. After being criticized for our failure to reduce domestic child poverty, we haven't submitted a five-year report since 2001.

This doesn't mean we can't renew our commitment to children now. After reading through this selection of columns, we hope you find a story that inspires you to take action the way Iqbal inspired us. We are firm believers that you are never too young to change the world – asking for a commitment to children's rights is a great place to start.

School should enlighten,
not indoctrinate
November 12, 2007

An educational revolution is underway in the world's largest democracy.

As students in India returned to class this year, they were greeted by a radical new approach to teaching in the country's schools – one that may change how an entire generation sees its country and the world.

With a new curriculum and textbooks introduced by the government's National Council of Educational Research and Training, students in both the public and private systems will now begin taking a much more honest look at contemporary Indian politics.

Gone are the days when education in India meant simply memorizing a textbook written to suit the views of the ruling political party. Now everything is fair game – from Indira Gandhi's highly controversial emergency rule in the 1970s to attacks on Muslims in Gujarat just five years ago.

One of the textbooks even encourages students to brainstorm and debate the elements of India's foreign policy that they would like to change.

"The old curriculum was not very focused on critical thinking," says Yohan Matthew, who studied in Mumbai until he was 13 before continuing his education in Canada. "It was a lot of memorization, there was no discussion."

That type of rote learning made independent thought especially difficult because the textbooks were often highly subjective.

"A majority of Indian students [had] their studies… in the language of the state. As a result the texts were biased to project the views of the state government," explains Amar Vyas, who studied in Uttar Pradesh and now lives in the United Kingdom.

While some worry that the new curriculum will be politicized, most acknowledge that if India is going to solidify its place as a major player on the world stage, it's going to have to educate students to think for themselves.

Having millions of youth as a captive audience five days a week means wielding incredible power over the way they think and act as adults. It's a power that India has started using to initiate constructive change. But in many other countries around the world, governments continue to take advantage of it, using school curriculum as a political tool.

In Russia, for example, a growing nostalgia for Stalinism has found its way into the classroom. A teaching manual released in June 2007 calls Joseph Stalin "the most successful leader of the U.S.S.R.," and downplays the 13 million people who were killed or sent to labour camps under his rule.

The text, partly authored by Vladimir Putin's chief political strategist, is already having an impact. A recent poll by the Yuri Levada Centre in Russia found that 54 per cent of youth believe Stalin did more good than bad while in power and that 50 per cent see him as a wise leader.

But nowhere has the power of curriculum had a greater and more brutal impact than in Sierra Leone. During the country's 11-year civil war, thousands of teachers were murdered by rebels in a violent attempt to indoctrinate the young.

The rebels, who saw teachers as "wisdom keepers," figured that without an education, children would be more susceptible to their anti-government ideology. So they went on a massive campaign targeting teachers and their schools.

That's the power of education.

Back in India, no one knows how long the new curriculum will last – the country's politicians have a long history of interfering in schools. But if the new lessons remain, they will symbolize a growing maturity in the world's largest democracy.

Not only will they prove that India is serious about its emerging international role, they will also ensure that the country's future is in well-educated, capable hands.

What a lesson that would be for the rest of the world.

Major differences still exist between the public and private school streams in India. Along with introducing improved textbooks, many still push to improve the country's education system. In March 2010, the Union Cabinet discussed five new bills that will hopefully reform and improve the higher education system.

Discussion Questions:

1. The article describes how, historically, textbooks in India were written to reflect the views of the government. What are the implications of this practice? Do you think this happens in Canada?
2. Think about all the sources of information in schools related to Canadian history. Do they create a critical thinking approach to history?

***

Closed doors in U.S. open a global market in education
September 1, 2008

Applying to university is stressful enough. Add waiting for a visa and the stress level skyrockets.

In 2003, Vibhor Gupta faced just that predicament when the student from New Delhi and his friends began applying for school abroad.

The United States came top-rated. The only problem was new immigration rules which restricted access to the country.

"Getting a visa is tough," says Gupta. "A lot of people I know applied for visas in other countries after they got rejected by the U.S."

With family in Canada, Gupta decided against applying in the United States altogether. He settled on the University of New Brunswick to study computer engineering. After graduation, he began working full-time at a Canadian tech firm.

Gupta is one of many international students who were dissuaded from applying in the United States. Following Sept. 11, visa denials and delays caused a decline in enrolment at U.S. universities. By 2003, growth in foreign student enrolment had fallen to one per cent after five consecutive years at five per cent.

In 2007, the growth in international student enrolment started to rebound, reaching three per cent. But these numbers aren't what they once were. It's because American universities are now facing more competition. When the United States closed its doors, other countries opened theirs.

"There are a number of countries that have started to expand their research university programs," says Kathie Bailey-Mathae, director of the Board of International Scientific Organizations at the National Academies. "It's no longer a few countries. It's really a global market."

The biggest barrier to obtaining a visa came from face-to-face interviews with an American consular officer. Always a requirement for students, when it was discovered that most of the Sept. 11 hijackers gained valid visas without interviews, the meetings became a requirement for everyone.

The result was months-long delays as long lines formed around U.S. embassies and applicants dealt with overworked interviewers.

"The start of the semester wasn't negotiable. Students had to wait when they had a date to be here by," says Bailey-Mathae.

While the international students waited in line, other countries capitalized on the opportunity. Canada, Britain and Australia adopted aggressive programs to attract the students. At the same time, emerging markets like India and China expanded their universities.

By 2001, the proportion of the world's PhDs granted in the U.S. had fallen from 54 per cent in the 1970s to 41 per cent, according to the National Academies. At the same time, China awarded 12 per cent of these degrees, compared to virtually zero 20 years ago.

This increase in global options combined with the tightening of U.S. security has deterred students from coming to the United States. What was an effort to increase physical security may be a blow to economic security.

In the education sector alone, the Institute of International Education says international students contribute $14.5 billion each year in tuition and living expenses.

As graduates, they stay in large numbers working for American companies. Their skills and their ties to their home countries have proven invaluable to multinational companies, especially in the technology and science sectors.

"Those ties between countries are very important," says Bailey-Mathae. "The experience and the cultural nuances that the foreign students bring really add to the opportunities for more balanced research."

The U.S. government has tried to make access easier for students by easing some laws and giving priority interviews. But, with more schools competing for the top students, the security measures have discouraged many from applying at all.

It's no longer Harvard versus Yale. The competition is now much larger.

"It's the global economy now and it's not what it was 10 years ago," says Bailey-Mathae. "Everyone is competing."

Discussion Questions:
1. What kinds of benefits can international students provide to the country in which they study? What would less international students mean to universities or the workforce?
2. Canada has a very small population relative to its size. The workforce is also getting older and many people are getting ready to retire. What would more international students now mean for the future?

✷✷✷

Your shirt off their backs
February 2, 2009

In a restaurant, we heard a common exchange. "Nice shirt," said one patron. "Where's it from?"

The fashionista offered a store name. We returned to our meals. The question lingered.

Where's it from? Not just this shirt. Any shirt. Look at your own label. Where's it from?

Chances are it went through numerous hands before ending up on your back. That's where the question takes new meaning. Where's it from? And, who's it from?

In the beginning, there was a child.

Crouched in a field in Uzbekistan, that child is most likely contributing to the primary industry of the second-largest cotton exporter in the world. Not because he wants to. Because he has to.

When cotton makes up 60 per cent of his country's export earnings, everyone is expected to pitch in. Through school closures and campaigns encouraging loyalty to the president and the country, the government sends children to the fields. In 2000, UNICEF estimated 22.6 per cent of kids aged five to 14 were harvesting the cotton. Some were even given plastic water bottles filled with pesticide to spray on the crop.

The most fortunate child gets three cents for every kilogram picked – a kilogram worth $1.15 on the world market.

The Uzbek government maintains that no child labour exists in their country. Still, come September, rather than heading to class, the children diligently pick the cotton, pack it up and ship it off.

Most countries that grow cotton – places like Uzbekistan – don't have their own textile industries. So, the T-shirt continues on its journey from the hands of a child to a manufacturer in China.

There, in massive factories the size of multiple football fields, machines spin the cotton into yarn while looms weave the soft fibre into fabric. It's a practice that used to belong to skilled craftsmen – artisans who took pride in delicately creating the fabric. Today, labourers paid cheap wages produce the cloth at discounted prices before passing it on to a woman in Bangladesh.

There, cotton textile manufacturing is king. About 4,000 garment factories fill the capital of Dhaka and employ 2.5 million people, mostly women.

The woman making our specific T-shirt arrives at work at five a.m. and spends 13 hours at her sewing machine. She is surrounded by younger workers, some under the legal working age of 13, who hem her seams and finish the item off.

The woman makes about $25 monthly – the government-mandated minimum wage – barely enough to afford food and her squalid living conditions.

Still, she works without complaint. Her fear is conditions getting better. The company might leave Bangladesh for a place with more lenient laws. If that happens, she would face unemployment, hunger and potentially prostitution to keep her family afloat.

So, she finishes the T-shirt and passes it on for its journey across the Pacific Ocean. Into the hands of dockworkers, the shirt is loaded into 40-foot shipping containers and sent to North America. Then, in the back of a tractor-trailer, it's driven across the country to your local mall where it's unloaded and placed on a rack by a teenager.

That teen likely gets minimum wage, ranging from $8.00 per hour in British Columbia to $10.25 in Ontario.

From there, the item is bought – one of about 1.4 billion cotton T-shirts sold annually in North America. It's pulled over a head. It's thrown in the wash. It begs the question, "Where's it from?"

The short answer would be the store in the mall. But the short answer neither tells us the whole story nor makes us informed consumers.

T-shirts don't just magically appear on hangers. Chances are they've crossed more borders than you.

Discussion Questions:
1. How often do you and your family look at the country listed on clothing tags? Should this influence your purchase decision?
2. Think from the perspective of the workers mentioned in this column. Why do they continue to work under these conditions?

✱✱✱

Teaching the unspeakable in Rwanda
April 6, 2009

In a Kigali classroom, a Rwandan child raises his hand to answer the teacher's question.

It's remarkable he's even there. Fifteen years ago, the genocide not only left 800,000 dead, it also left the education system in tatters. Over 600 classrooms were destroyed and 75 per cent of teachers were either killed or imprisoned.

As anniversaries passed, those schools were rebuilt with incredible speed. New teachers were trained and students flooded the classrooms. Eagerly, they learned – just not what you'd expect.

Amidst the brightly-coloured uniforms and texts on math, science and English, there's no mention of genocide. That's been the norm since 1994 when the government placed a moratorium on its teaching.

The reasoning is straightforward. History manipulation fuelled the genocide. So, the government disallowed its teaching until consensus was reached on how to do it right.

Fifteen years later, that consensus has yet to be reached. And, the subject's absence is doing little to help the healing.

"Kids are absorbing the subject everywhere. It's not like people aren't talking about it around them," says Karen Murphy, director of international programs at Facing History, an organization that develops educational material for post-conflict countries. "The question becomes what does the school system do when they have students coming in with all kinds of versions of the events?"

It's a scary thought – but one that Murphy's organization is taking on.

About 42 per cent of Rwandans were born after the genocide. Although about 10 per cent of the population was killed in 1994, it quickly recovered as birth rates steadily rose, resting at about 5.25 children per woman in 2009.

Despite having no direct memory of the genocide, it's nearly impossible for them to escape it. Memorials have popped up around the country and bullet holes still scar the parliament's walls. It's not uncommon to see a survivor with a missing limb in the street or the pink uniforms that identify prisoners in the back of pickup trucks.

As government programs and international aid deal with the myriad post-genocide problems from infrastructure to orphans, the history of the 100 days that caused those problems has largely been accounted for in movies like *Hotel Rwanda* or books like *Shake Hands with the Devil*. They're popular here in North America but not nearly as accessible in the country that inspired them.

In 2003, Murphy, in partnership with the University of California, Berkeley set out to change that. Together with the National University of Rwanda and the Ministry of Education, they began tackling the history question.

"There is a lot of shame and humiliation when it comes to teaching the genocide," says Murphy. "Teachers need to create safety – a space for kids to learn about their own violent past and the rest of the world."

By training teachers to facilitate debate and developing educator resources, the partnership has created a model for teaching. The trick is to use case studies of the Holocaust, apartheid, Bosnia and even the civil rights movement. Murphy explains this takes away the personal connection.

Instead of focusing on what happened to or what was perpetrated by the children's parents, the resources connect them to the greater humanity.

"Sometimes young people are better able to make connections through the distance of another case study than by shining a bright light on their own history," says Murphy. "Then they recognize it's not just a Rwandan problem."

On the contrary, it's a problem that many others must wrestle themselves. South Africa must teach apartheid and Germany the Second World War. Closer to home, we must tackle our own demons with the civil rights movement in the United States and residential schools here in Canada.

Yes, mistakes were committed by everyone. But, it's in teaching those mistakes that the next generation can learn and work towards a better future.

Discussion Questions:
1. Why is it important to learn about past atrocities like the Rwandan genocide? Why is it sometimes easier to learn from events that happen in other countries as opposed to ones that occur in your own backyard?
2. Many believe it is important to learn from past mistakes in order to ensure we don't repeat them. If this is true, why didn't the lessons learned from the Holocaust prevent the Rwandan genocide?

India's children don't have vote — or clean water
May 18, 2009

Surmaal used to be an enthusiastic student in his third-grade classroom.

That was before his father passed away. Now, the 12-year-old is head of his household in the village of Lai, India. But, while he is shouldering an adult's responsibilities, Surmaal is still a child.

That made him too young to vote in the country's 2009 elections. His concerns went largely unnoticed.

For Surmaal and his family, getting water from the village hand pump is of vital importance. There are wells closer to his home but water depletion has caused them to run dry. So, Surmaal traverses two hills with the heavy buckets.

Like most people in the town, Surmaal would love to see those wells put back into use. That way, he could attend school again.

But, without a vote, it is not a high political priority. Water gets overshadowed by the economy and national defence. By ignoring this issue which is affecting India's most vulnerable population, the world's largest democracy isn't really addressing its nation's challenges.

"It's baffling that something so fundamental to people's lives is way down the list of political priorities for all countries," says Tom Palakudiyil, head of Asia region at WaterAid. "There is a huge amount of loss by not giving water and sanitation the attention it needs."

The coordination of India's election is nothing short of extraordinary. It's a feat that involves thousands of candidates, five phases of voting and polling stations that eliminate geographic barriers for the country's 700 million eligible voters.

That's incredible coordination, but something that doesn't translate to water. India still lacks sanitation facilities for about 700 million people. On top of that, 200 million don't have access to drinking water. Those that do have no guarantee it is actually safe.

Still, water tends to get overlooked.

"Within the cities where the affluent voters are, water is not such an issue," says Palakudiyil. "This issue touches the poor families. That's a vast number but it doesn't automatically translate into political dialogue."

The problem is that those being affected the most are not among the eligible voters – the children like Surmaal.

Surmaal is not alone in missing school to bring water to his mother and younger sisters. Millions like him perform the same chores each day. All are at risk of waterborne illnesses like typhoid, dysentery and diarrhea. In fact, one in nine children will die before their fifth birthday largely due to illnesses like this.

But, it doesn't have to be this way. The solutions to India's water problems are within grasp. It just takes a coordinated effort to actually make it happen.

"Where people have systematically gone about taking actions to regenerate water in a region, after two or three years of community efforts, there is greenery and wells start to hold water again," says Palakudiyil. "If the communities come together, we can improve the water and keep it safe."

While a move towards better water infrastructure is more long-term, there are options to help alleviate the water shortage now.

The communities in which Palakudiyil works have been able to conserve water through rainwater harvesting and educational efforts. As well, point-of-use water purification tablets can eliminate the risk of disease. Currently, these tablets are not widely available. But, through increased distribution efforts, these effective and inexpensive treatments could be sold at shops and kiosks in towns across the country.

These solutions are doable. We just need the political will to stand up for those like Surmaal who don't have a vote. India successfully coordinated an election involving 700 million participants. Now, it needs to put that effort into bringing them water.

Discussion Questions:

1. If there are 700 million people eligible to vote in India and 200 million don't have access to clean water, why do you think that this issue is not at the top of the political agenda?

2. What are some issues affecting youth that you would like to see discussed in Canadian elections? Should the legal age of voting be lowered so that more young people are able to cast a ballot?

A bank run by street kids, for street kids
October 19, 2009

To find a bank still readily giving loans during the financial crisis, you need only look as far as a New Delhi train station.

There you'll find a child sitting at a ramshackle post. Despite his unkempt appearance, he's branch manager. Expertly trained by the people at Butterflies, a New Delhi-based children's charity, he diligently takes deposits and marks them down in his client's passbook.

Like many banks, there's fine-print. All clients must be below the age of 18.

The Children's Development Khazana is unlike traditional banking institutions. You won't find many suits among their elected board of governors. That's because it's completely run by street kids.

With 26 main branches and 53 sub-branches across India, Afghanistan, Bangladesh, Nepal, Kyrgyzstan and Sri Lanka, the Khazana gives more than the opportunity to save their money – it gives children the opportunity to invest in their futures.

"In Hindi, *khazana* means wealth. We liked how that sounds. 'Children's development wealth,'" says Gerry Pinto, an advisor for Butterflies. "We brought it to the kids for discussion, they took to it."

Wealth isn't easy for street children to accumulate. Their earnings first buy food. Then there is real concern of losing it. Extra money is often spent on destructive pastimes like drug abuse or gambling. It may also be stolen by older kids, policemen and others in positions of power. Sometimes shopkeepers who agree to take care of the money never give it back.

Observing this, Butterflies offered sanctuary for the children's money. Once they had gathered enough, that collective piggybank became a place of business.

"They said they didn't want to go to a real bank," says Pinto. "They said, 'Big banks do not respect us because we are not dressed well. We want our own.'"

They came up with a system of passbooks and account

numbers to record earnings. Then, they elected child managers and committees who trained with Butterflies in accounting to keep track of the day-to-day banking. The other children are then invited to basic literacy, math and budget training to better keep track of their deposits and withdrawals.

To take out a loan, they must draft a proposal to start a business or go back to school, and submit it for approval by the loan committee.

"We help them through the whole process of appointing a board of directors and a child manager," says Pinto. "It teaches them democratic practices, how to organize a meeting and how to budget for expenses."

That in turn helps the children plan for their futures.

Take Tania Naaz for example. The 17-year-old daughter of a sex worker living in Muzaffarpur, India learned embroidery skills to make a living but had nowhere to put her earnings. After her father was paralyzed in an accident, she felt pressure to join her mother's profession in order to provide for the family – until she opened an account at the Khazana.

Naaz began making regular deposits. After a year, she took out a loan of 5,000 rupees and started her own business. Since then, she has actually paid back 2,200 rupees of her loan, saved another 1,250 in her account and avoided exploitation in the sex trade.

"The major element that attracts children is making money," says Pinto. "But, when it comes to capturing their minds and promoting these development ideas, there is nothing like the bank."

Pinto explains they have seen hundreds of children break through poverty by saving. One group of children in Sri Lanka even used their collective earnings to construct girls' toilets for the community.

While none of the children with accounts at the Khazana seem like the most desirable candidates for a loan, the opportunities created by an account and passbook are seemingly endless.

That's because investing in someone's future is never a risk.

Discussion Questions:
1. Imagine that you are a bank manager at a children's bank. How would you persuade another young person to deposit money?
2. Could a model that helps street youth or young people living below the poverty line work in Canada? Why or why not?

✳✳✳

World's adults must honour vow to children
November 16, 2009

It speaks to the values of our society when we can't protect our most vulnerable citizens – our children.

Twenty years ago, the United Nations adopted the Convention on the Rights of the Child (UNCRC). Since then, it has been ratified by 193 countries including every UN Member State, but the United States and Somalia. This was the first document to enshrine children's rights not as someone's daughter or son, but as distinct members of our society requiring special protection and rights.

The document itself was revolutionary. The support was unprecedented – the most widely ratified convention in history. The UNCRC laid out the civil, cultural, economic, political and social rights for children. Around the world, it was hailed for the solemn promise it made for protecting children and the hope it represented for our future.

We came together. We promised. Twenty years later, it's clear we failed.

There's a tendency to look at UN legislation as simply a piece of paper. But the UNCRC represents much more. Each article lays out a challenge facing a child somewhere in the world. Each article also lays out the potential for real change in that child's life.

The rights in the document were laid out in three categories known as the three P's – provision, protection and participation.

Provision is embodied by Mirian who lives in San Miguel, Ecuador. The rights under this section of the convention were supposed to guarantee her basic needs in life including a standard of living, education and health care. But Mirian has not been able to attend school as her family cannot afford the cost.

Protection represents the kids who find their way to the Children of War Rehabilitation Center in Gulu, Uganda. Under this section of the convention, these kids were supposed to be kept safe from harm including kidnapping, child labour, sexual exploitation and war. Yet, over 15,000 of these kids have made their way through the rehabilitation centre after being used as soldiers, sex slaves and servants in the country's ongoing conflict.

Participation is Surmaal from Lai, in Rajasthan, India. He is supposed to be guaranteed a say in the matters affecting his life. But, despite the fact that the 12-year-old became the male head of his household after his father died, Surmaal has little say regarding his country's issues with water supply. Right now, he can't pursue his education because he spends his day walking long distances to collect water for his family.

But, on the twentieth anniversary of the UNCRC, we can put these children at the forefront.

United States President Barack Obama has already acknowledged the embarrassment of finding his country alongside a virtually ungoverned Somalia in holding out on ratification.

The convention was signed by former president Bill Clinton in 1995. But, it has yet to be approved by Congress as many assert it infringes on domestic policy-making, particularly with military recruitment and treatment of minors by courts.

The current policy of sentencing people to life imprisonment without parole for crimes committed as juveniles violates the UNCRC. But one obstacle was removed in 2005 when the Supreme Court ruled these prisoners could not receive the death penalty. Now, further measures must be taken to address these issues and move forward with ratification.

Canada also has significant shortcomings. After criticism from the UN on inaction related to domestic child poverty, the government ceased filing reports for review. It has failed to submit a five-year annual document since 2001.

The 20th anniversary of the UNCRC is the perfect time for Canada and the world to renew our commitment to children.

Canada can start by submitting to a review, learning from the criticism and actually implementing the policies.

Any good parent teaches their children not to lie. It's time that adults acted by example and lived up to our promise.

Discussion Questions:

1. To what extent do you think issues relating to young people are taken seriously in your community? Your country?
2. If governments aren't making progress in implementing the UNCRC, what can young people do to defend the rights of their peers worldwide?

***

Cycle of poverty, violence keep children from realizing dreams
February 15, 2010

When Beatriz drew a picture of what she wants to be when she grows up, the 11-year-old sketched a policewoman.

She drew a smiling face with *polecia* written underneath. Hearts, stars and open-toothed grins created a border.

It's quite the dream growing up in Ciudad Juarez, Mexico. Most of the criminals she will fight belong to drug cartels contributing to increasing levels of violence, corruption and murder. If Beatriz gets an education, not only could she defeat them, she could also pull her parents and 11 brothers and sisters from crippling poverty.

Sadly, despite her capabilities, it's the same violence and poverty she wants to fight that could keep Beatriz from school. It's also what will hold the entire region in a vicious cycle.

"Often there are large families and a lot of kids. They can't feed themselves so their parents can't afford to send everyone to school," says Charlene Golding who runs a U.S.-based organization called Juarez Kids with her daughter Caroline. "By nine years of age, they need to work to bring home money."

For some, that money will come from factory work. Others will

34

choose the drug trade.

On a mission to Juarez in 2007, Golding and her daughter met Beatriz amid what they call "the war next door." Within 20 minutes of the El Paso, Texas border, they were confronted by families living in homes made of cardboard with no running water or electricity.

On top of this, they learned Beatriz needed between $125 and $165 for tuition, uniform and books as education isn't free. This was too much for her parents. They are among many poor families who migrated to the border region in search of low-paying factory jobs.

The Goldings began fundraising for scholarships. Around the world, education has proven to be a crucial factor in fighting poverty. If Beatriz had money for school, she could fulfill her dream, support her family and create a better life for her own children. But, when their next trip was cancelled for security reasons, it became clear financial security can't provide physical security.

Last year, over 2,600 murders occurred in Juarez, up from 1,600 in 2008. About 134 minors were killed in the crossfire as rival drug cartels strove for power. The situation is such that on Oct. 30, a local newspaper announced the first murder-free day in 10 months.

"At this point you wonder are these kids even safe?" says Golding. "When they are sending in troops and there's extortion going on, education is great but we're talking about are these kids even safe at this point?"

Children are increasingly drawn into what can only be described as war. Many schools are forced to close when classrooms are held hostage and kids used as tools for extortion. As well, young people are increasingly being recruited as active participants in crime.

They have little choice. The Juarez Chamber of Commerce says 6,000 businesses closed in 2009. With kids expected to help their family earn a living, they are forced to choose between $10 per day in a factory job and potentially $500 for one drug smuggling trip. With more and more innocent bystanders being killed, virtually the same level of physical danger is carried by school, factory and criminality.

Police at one border crossing recently reported a 13-year-old in a car filled with drugs. As young people get more involved in the trade, this only perpetuates the violence keeping kids out of school and families in poverty.

"It's almost as if an educational issue turned into a humanitarian crisis," says Golding. "What's so shocking is this is happening right across our border."

With 2009 setting a record for its level of violence, Golding can only hope that Beatriz stays safe.

Hopefully, when she's old enough, she can fulfill her dream of stopping the violence.

Discussion Questions:

1. Think about your childhood experiences and future plans and compare to the children described in the column. What options do youth in Canada have to help address the root causes?

2. The column suggests that education could help pull families out of poverty. How does this happen? What would have to change in this community in order to allow kids like Beatriz to get an education?

2
Child Soldiers

Over the past few years, we've had the pleasure of working with a young man named Michel Chikwanine.

Michel grew up in the Democratic Republic of Congo, a wartorn country in central Africa. As a child, he was kidnapped, drugged and trained as a child soldier.

At 11, Michel left his home country as a refugee, eventually settling in Canada. Today, he travels the country delivering motivational speeches with a message that true happiness can only be achieved by helping others.

We are constantly amazed by Michel's courage, understanding and ability to touch lives. But, the sad fact remains that he is one of thousands of children around the world who have unfairly been pulled into the frontlines of war.

Child-soldiering is not the only way in which children have been influenced by conflict. Along with those fighting on the frontlines, there are girls used as sex slaves and labourers who carry equipment and supplies. In total, there are an estimated 300,000 children working with fighting forces in 36 countries. They often leave the armies malnourished, uneducated and with severe emotional and physical wounds. Each has been placed into a situation most adults will never have to face.

Child soldiers have come up numerous times during the last four years of Global Voices. In the following series of articles, we hope to broaden your perspective on this issue through the stories of kids just like Michel who have found themselves trapped in conflict.

In the first, a young man named John Mafinder calls for justice for child soldiers on the eve of the trial of a warlord named Charles Taylor at the International Criminal Court. Taylor, the former President of Liberia, has been accused of war crimes including the use of child soldiers. At the time of this book's publication, that trial was still in progress, more than three years after the column was originally printed.

Then, there is the story of Omar Khadr, who at 15, was arrested in Afghanistan and charged with war crimes for allegedly throwing a grenade that killed a U.S. soldier. We hope that by reading this column you will question why this young man wasn't considered a child soldier and question your own government on their attitudes toward the practice. Finally, we hope the last column highlights that while physical wounds heal, emotional wounds are much more complicated. For child soldiers themselves, the atrocities they have seen can leave deep scars. For the communities who have suffered because of the armies they were once a part of, forgiveness doesn't come easy.

This is why we felt child soldiers deserved their own section in this compilation. The scars they face are something few adults can comprehend. Helping them fade is a community effort.

Just verdict for forcing kids to fight
July 2, 2007

Out of the tiny country of Sierra Leone has come a huge victory for human rights.

The recent conviction of three of its former rebel fighters for recruiting and using child soldiers was truly historic. The first of its kind by a United Nations court, this landmark decision sends a clear message that anyone who turns children into killers will not escape justice.

Indeed, the message is long overdue. Around the globe, more than 300,000 children are in combat – from Colombia to Sri Lanka – in what is one of the world's worst forms of exploitation.

Up until now, those responsible for it have escaped prosecution. But that is beginning to change.

The precedent comes just as former Liberian president Charles Taylor goes on trial for war crimes in The Hague. He is accused of orchestrating Sierra Leone's 11-year civil war by funding the rebel army known for forcing children to murder their families, mutilate villagers and engage in ritualistic acts of cannibalism.

Taylor faces 11 war crimes charges – including the conscription of child soldiers. Once feared throughout West Africa for his brutality, he is the first African head of state to face such charges.

Taylor has long denied the charges against him, saying he "did not and could not" have played a role in Sierra Leone's war.

But the child soldiers tell a different story.

On our most recent visit to Sierra Leone, we met John Mafinder, a 15-year-old former soldier who was captured by rebels at the age of 12. Despite being too young to lift anything heavier than a pistol, he spent more than a year as the bodyguard for a senior rebel nicknamed Rambo.

Skinny and shy but with a look of exhaustion and bags under his eyes, he had never opened up to anyone about his life as a soldier – not even to his family – until we met him in the wartorn Kono District.

John and his friends were captured by rebels as they fled the country. Those who were too small for combat were immediately killed, while the others were turned into soldiers.

He explained how he was trained by Liberian mercenaries to raid villages, amputate and murder locals and use heavy weaponry. Children who refused were beaten.

The weapons, from handguns to AK-47s, were flown by helicopter from Liberia. John told us they would be brought by English-speaking white men who were often paid in diamonds.

He says the shipments – as many as six per day – were arranged by senior rebels and Liberian officials. John remembers the rebels being in regular contact with supporters in Liberia, including with Charles Taylor himself.

In fact, on one occasion he even saw Taylor spend the night at his rebel commander's home.

John's firsthand experiences, as well as those of many other child soldiers we spoke to, add to the evidence indicating that the Liberian warlord did collaborate with rebels in Sierra Leone.

The war in this small West African country was one of the most horrific in recent memory, especially for the 10,000 or more children like John who were given drugs – often a mix of cocaine and gunpowder called "brown brown" – to induce a kill or be killed mentality. Many have been scarred for life.

For too long though, rebels and dictators who arm children have found impunity. That is why the legal precedent set in Sierra Leone is so important – it ensures that war's youngest victims are not forgotten.

So as the world turns its attention to the trial of Charles Taylor, the stories of these children must be told. While they have had the tragic misfortune of bearing witness to atrocities, they also have the power to bring perpetrators to justice.

Discussion Questions:

1. Why do leaders who use child soldiers rarely receive punishment?
2. If Charles Taylor is convicted of war crimes at the International Criminal Court, do you think this will help John Mafinder find justice?

A Canadian child soldier
July 21, 2008

Their stories are all too shocking, yet all too familiar.

In Sierra Leone, boys as young as 10 were turned into bloodthirsty soldiers through an injection called "brown brown," a mixture of cocaine and gunpowder used to induce fits of rage and violence. In Sri Lanka, rebels strapped suicide-bomb belts to children with the assumption that police would never suspect an innocent child.

All around the world, child soldiers like these have been forced into combat. From Congo to Colombia, some 300,000 kids are at war, often against their will. Their exploitation is among the most severe, as physical, emotional and sexual abuse is used to force young boys and girls to do unimaginable things.

The world acknowledges their plight and recognizes the fact that a child's mind is far too impressionable to stand up to the forces of hatred and manipulation. That's why multiple international treaties call for child soldiers to be rehabilitated – not imprisoned. It's a standard upheld in even the deadliest war zones.

Then there is the case of Omar Khadr.

Spending part of his childhood in Afghanistan and Pakistan, he was no stranger to violent ideology. Khadr's larger-than-life father was a friend of Osama bin Laden and often glorified violence and martyrdom, instructing his six children that such death and destruction were the only worthy pursuits in life.

His father once tried to convince an elder son to become a suicide bomber and even threatened to kill all of his kids if they ever betrayed his fundamentalist version of Islam. By 10, Khadr had received his first weapons training.

It's no wonder the boy who teachers once described as "very smart, very eager and very polite" became fanatical like his father.

But unlike other children forced into war, post-conflict Khadr has been thrown in jail, left to languish and even abused, as a Canadian government report revealed in July 2008. Despite being only 15 at the time of his arrest by U.S. forces in eastern Afghanistan, Khadr is charged with war crimes and expected to stand trial in October.

Why is he treated so differently from other child soldiers? The answer is clearly political.

Imagine if he had been caught fighting anywhere else or by anyone else. The brainwashing he suffered at the hands of the man he trusted most would illicit unwavering sympathy. He would be cared for as the United Nation, International Labour Organization and other organizations require, and certainly wouldn't be jailed with a bunch of adults.

In Sierra Leone, for example, former child soldiers participate in elaborate forgiveness rituals aimed at reintroducing them into their villages. In places like Rwanda, they are demilitarized and even given job training.

It's an incredible injustice that a Canadian-born child in American custody is not afforded the same rights. If you remove the politics of the situation and look at Khadr's case on moral grounds, it becomes obvious that his special treatment is inexcusable.

Canada's hands are far from clean. While Britain and Australia negotiated to have their own citizens repatriated from the prison at Guantanamo Bay, Canada refuses to intervene. Khadr is the only Westerner still jailed there. He's also the youngest.

Both Canada and the United States need to treat Khadr no differently than other child soldiers, starting by returning him to Canada. If he is tried and convicted, it will set a terrible international precedent that threatens the hundreds of thousands of other children around the world who have been manipulated into war.

Putting a child soldier in jail is not justice. Rehabilitating him from the shackles of his exploitation is.

At the time of publication, Khadr remained the youngest prisoner in Guantanamo Bay as well as the only Westerner. In Jan. 2010, he lost a Supreme Court bid that would have forced Canadian Prime Minister Stephen Harper to ask the U.S. to repatriate Khadr. He has yet to face trial for his alleged crimes although a military commission was scheduled for the summer of 2010. The location of this hearing, whether in Cuba or the United States, has yet to be determined. Reports have circulated in the Canadian media that the U.S. hopes to avoid trying a child soldier for war crimes and is quietly looking for a way to repatriate Khadr to Canada.

Discussion Questions:
1. Despite the fact that Khadr was under 18 when he was captured, he wasn't treated as a child soldier. Why? What makes his case different from other child soldiers?
2. What are the similarities and differences between Khadr's story and that of John Mafinder in the previous article?

***

Former child soldiers face psychological battle
May 4, 2009

The egg represents purity.

It is untouched, unscathed and innocent. Then, it is stepped on. The innocence is crushed. It sits broken and exposed.

The symbolism of the event is not lost on the Acholi people of northern Uganda. The ceremony is an important step in reintegrating and cleansing someone who has been away from the community for a long period of time. After 22 years of war, the Acholi have been doing this a lot for child soldiers.

They left as children – pure and innocent like the egg. But they come back psychologically broken even if they are still physically young.

They are children forcibly recruited by fighting forces. For them and the communities they return to, these ceremonies are essential for everyone to move forward.

Worldwide, an estimated 300,000 kids in 36 countries have had their childhoods replaced by horrors no person should have to endure.

Their outer wounds are easy to fix. But, the process of rehabilitation and giving them a new life is complicated and requires personal and cultural forgiveness.

"Any child that has experienced this, the memories will never leave them," says Dirk Booy, executive director of World Vision Canada which runs the Children of War Rehabilitation Center in Gulu, Uganda. "It will impact them for the rest of their lives."

The conflict between Ugandan government forces and the Lord's Resistance Army is older than most of the child soldiers fighting the battles. In the last two decades, an estimated 25,000 children have been abducted for use as fighters, sex slaves and labourers. Although, some estimates put that number closer to 66,000.

"All of them have experienced different atrocities," says Booy. "The army has beaten them and forced them to watch other violent acts to desensitize them. Then, they engage in the acts themselves for fear of their lives."

Since opening its doors in 1995, the Children of War Center has helped rehabilitate 15,000 children associated with fighting forces. Booy explains the first step is to address the immediate needs – food, shelter and medical attention. Then, they move on to the psychological wounds.

"They come to us traumatized, stigmatized, some of them experienced signs of post-traumatic stress," says Booy. "The centre works with them on these issues helping them draw out their experiences and get back to a normal routine."

These psychological approaches are essential to the healing process. Using counselling sessions, art and acting, the children are encouraged to talk about their experiences. These are often brutal stories of torture, forced killings, drugs and fighting. Even if the child never held a gun themselves, they often speak of sexual abuse, servitude and forced labour.

But just as important are the cultural practices. The egg ceremony has a distinct purpose in acknowledging the foreign elements that crushed the community and the child. In addition, the child must jump over two twigs. The first, called the *layibi*, is used to open the granary, symbolizing a return to where one once ate. The second, from the opobo tree is traditionally used to make soap. It represents cleansing.

While the tradition is much different from the counselling we often use in the Western world, the rituals work to make the former combatant feel safe and welcomed back into the community.

"We conduct them in a very public way with the community members in order to re-establish the kids and reintegrate them," says Booy. "We need the kids to feel good about themselves, who they are and how the community feels about them."

That's a process that's not easy to anyone – community, counsellor or child. Despite some of the best treatment in the world, we can never give someone back their childhood.

While their physical wounds will heal, it's the deeper, internal scars that will live on.

Discussion Questions:
1. Why are the ceremonies described in the column held publicly? Why is it important for the community to be involved in reintegration?
2. If Omar Khadr received counselling and a similar ceremony was held, do you think Canadians would be willing to reintegrate him back into society?

3
Women's Rights

There's a reason why the water walk is almost always described as the most humbling experience on one of Me to We's volunteer trips to Kenya.

It's not the murky brown water that resembles something closer to chocolate milk than the stuff that runs from our taps at home. Neither is it the hour-long hike back to camp with a heavy jug strapped to your back and the hot sun beating down overhead.

Instead, it's the Mamas.

Each water walk is led by a woman from the Maasai Mara community who brings volunteers down to the river, helps them place the heavy loads on their backs and coaches them on the arduous journey home.

All the while, she explains how this walk isn't just an experience. It's a daily routine for the women in her village – a chore that's vital to the subsistence of families.

Over the years, we've seen participants ranging from students to business leaders realize that the burden of the heavy jug is nothing compared to the burden carried by the woman walking beside them. Her load is a much heavier and involves a multitude of tasks essential to keeping her family afloat.

Around the world, we've met many other women like the

Mamas in Kenya. There are grandmothers taking in orphans who have lost their parents to disease or disaster and mothers at stalls in the marketplace selling homemade goods for a little extra money that just might contribute to a brighter future for their children.

All too often, they are performing these essential tasks while being denied some very basic rights.

Women's rights is a subject that has been repeatedly broached through Global Voices. But, while it's a common thread that runs through each of the selected columns, we think you'll find the topics discussed are much more broad in nature. The issues range from condemning systematic oppression in Saudi Arabia to calling attention to gender-based violence in the Democratic Republic of Congo to looking at support for immigrant women who are about to have a baby here in North America.

These topics cover a wide spectrum of issues and no country is mentioned more than once. This is no accident. Women's rights is a truly global topic that ties directly into larger issues like poverty, development, the economy, even the environment.

Later on in this book, you will read a column about a drought taking place across the Maasai Mara region of Kenya. This means that the water walk is getting much longer for both our volunteer participants and, more importantly, the Mamas who guide them.

A longer walk means less time for the multitude of other tasks these women perform each day. It also means a much heavier burden.

Remorseful father fights to stop rape in South Africa
November 24, 2008

Dumisani Rebombo is protective of his daughters.

He wants them to be happy and marry men who will treat them well. It's a dream most fathers have. But in South Africa, according to the country's Commission on Gender Equality, a woman is raped every 17 seconds.

Rebombo knows this too well. That's why he wants to make sure his daughters don't meet someone like his younger self.

"In my youth, my friends and I, we gang-raped a girl in the village where I was growing up," he says.

It's a shocking statement to hear – especially from a man like Rebombo. The 47-year-old is at the forefront of the fight for gender equity in Africa, travelling the continent teaching men about sexual health and violence against women.

Rebombo knows he can't run from his past. So, despite the painful memories, he uses that past to change his daughters' present.

Rebombo grew up in South Africa under apartheid. The extreme repression and terror witnessed during this period left a legacy sociologists have described as a "culture of violence" which has contributed to attitudes accepting of sexual assault.

"Here, most men are still in a dominating position," he says. "The traditional leaders are all guys. We live in a patriarchy."

The rape he committed was accepted among the boys in the community. Rebombo was applauded, even given a pat on the back. Afterwards, he went on with his life, not thinking about the incident. Rebombo grew up and moved away. He married, had daughters. He got a job working at a clinic focused on HIV prevention.

There, it wasn't the life-threatening disease that had the most profound impact on Rebombo. It was the black eyes. Every week, Rebombo would see the scars and listen to the stories of beatings, rapes and abuse.

In each story, Rebombo saw the woman from his youth.

"I began to personalize the pain of the survivors," he says. "I talked with my pastor about how I felt the need to apologize to the woman I had raped. The pastor said, 'What if she goes to the authorities?' That didn't matter. I needed to give her justice."

Rebombo travelled 650 kilometres back to his village, hoping to clear his conscience. He asked around and found the woman. Like him, she was married, had children.

But, she hadn't forgotten the rape.

"She looked at me and she cried," says Rebombo. "Then, she said two other men after me had done the same thing."

Rebombo may have been the woman's first rape, but he wasn't her last. In the following years, she had survived two other vicious attacks. Rebombo was stunned. The woman explained she couldn't stand the thought of her husband touching her. She said she was emotionally unstable, her life destroyed.

"I realized for 20 years I was living this flamboyant life but here was a person who was struggling because of what I did," he says. "I left the village with a much heavier sentence.

"I knew I didn't want this to happen to my daughters."

Rebombo knew he couldn't constantly watch over the girls. So, he set about trying to prevent rape from happening. Through EngenderHealth's Men As Partners program, he began teaching men about gender stereotypes, taking active roles in family planning and advocating for women.

"No matter where you are, we can't have true democracy or true freedom when women can't walk alone in the streets," he says.

Now, from dirt-floored classrooms in rural villages to formal conferences with world dignitaries, Rebombo shares his story with a new purpose – that other men will learn from his mistakes.

That, he hopes, will protect his own and South Africa's daughters.

Discussion Questions:
1. What is your first impression of Dumisani Rebombo? How does your opinion of him change as you read through the story?
2. Rebombo explains how he needed to "give justice" to the woman he raped. Do you think that an apology would give her justice?

Times changing, but Saudi women still held back

May 11, 2009

The topic of our speech at the Saudi Arabian conference was about bringing society together through volunteerism.

That's why it seemed ironic a screen separated men and women in the audience.

Genders were also divided at dinner. During breakout sessions. Everywhere.

We spoke with some incredible women. Though we could only see their eyes through the black *abaya* cloak, they were filled with expression as they discussed their ideas and plans for grassroots volunteerism and civic engagement.

Too bad they couldn't share those ideas with their male counterparts.

The men told us, "Things are changing."

True. The country got a taste of equality in February when Nour al-Fayez was appointed the first female member of the Saudi Council of Ministers. But, that taste is bittersweet. Her position as Deputy Minister for Women's Education exists because of gender-segregated education.

That's if the girls even get an education. During our trip, a Saudi judge refused for a second time to annul an eight-year-old girl's marriage to a 47-year-old man.

He said she could petition for divorce after puberty.

Still, those men are right. Things are changing.

Oil prices have fallen and the financial crisis has devastated Western markets. The insecurity of Saudi Arabia's vast wealth became clear. To maintain its global status, Saudi needs to diversify. Not just its economy, but its workforce. It needs to unshackle its female population and embrace its potential.

"Women of Saudi Arabia, in full respect of their societal values, appear ready to embark on a new stage of engagement," said Yakin Ertürk, the Special Rapporteur of the United Nations Human Rights Council on Violence Against Women after a 2008 visit. "Supporting them on their endeavour requires vision, courage, leadership and a firm commitment from the highest levels of the state."

It's well-known Saudi Arabia's global status is derived from oil. But in 2008, we Westerners felt the scourge of our oil addiction when prices broke $145 per barrel. We're down from the peak but U.S. President Barack Obama has vowed to break our habit through alternatives.

A scary thought for Saudi Arabia – but one they are addressing.

As part of the "sun belt," Saudi Arabia has potential in future renewable energy markets. But, it wants to go beyond energy and develop the knowledge sector. So, it expanded the private sector and invested $7 billion in the Knowledge Economic City, a community near Medina, which is poised to create 20,000 jobs in the industrial, academic, cultural and commercial sectors.

It also invested in education. Saudi boasts the highest paid academics in the world with an average monthly salary of $6,611, and opened 12 new universities and colleges in the last four years. The Minister of Higher Education says they need 10 more to absorb the 70,000 students who currently study abroad.

But a knowledge-based economy requires human capital – and Saudi Arabia is only tapping half.

Gender discrimination in Saudi Arabia is described as sexual apartheid. About half of university graduates are women but less than a tenth have jobs. They cannot drive and must receive permission from male relatives to work, travel, study and marry.

"According to some professional women and officials, this prevents women from participating in the full range of activities and opportunities of the work environment and results in duplication of tasks as well as human and financial resources," said Ertürk in her report.

What Saudi Arabia isn't seeing is potential. We had that pleasure in our conference. But, we've also seen it on the world stage. Women across Saudi Arabia have shown their capabilities by fighting their own oppressive government for their own human rights.

Imagine what they could do if given the chance to fight for the rights of others.

The potential is there – it's just up to Saudi Arabia to recognize it.

Discussion Questions:

1. What is meant by the term "sexual apartheid?" What is the historical context behind using this term? What does the use of this term mean to you as a reader?
2. In what ways is the life of a Saudi Arabian woman different from yours? How would you react if you were denied certain rights and freedoms because of your gender?

✱✱✱

Rape, war and your cell phone
June 1, 2009

"I'm here." Two little words that sat in the inbox of one of our cell phones as we prepared to write this column.

This particular message came from a friend we met the evening prior. The room was crowded and she wanted to let us know, "I'm here."

Today, it seemed another woman wanted to tell us the same thing.

Her story is a little different. She is a survivor of rape. One so brutal she was torn apart – both physically and emotionally. The rape also succeeded in tearing apart her family, her village and now her country, the Democratic Republic of Congo.

Most people don't speak to this woman now. There's a lot of stigma attached to being raped by the soldiers of the rebel army controlling her region. The army is powerful, funded by the sale of minerals like tin, tantalum, tungsten and gold. Minerals that are shipped to Asia, made into electronic goods and sold to us in the form of cell phones.

Today, she sent us a message: "I'm here."

This woman's story is not unique in her country. In fact, about 1,100 rapes like hers are reported every month with countless more going unheard. Despite the United Nations naming the DRC the most dangerous place on earth to be a woman, little action has been taken to reverse this foreboding moniker.

The conflict in the Democratic Republic of Congo is ongoing

since 1996. An estimated 5.4 million people have died making it the deadliest conflict since World War II. Sexual violence has become a tool used by the militias to destroy communities.

"What the armies are trying to do is clear the land so they can take the resources," says Tanisha Taitt, producer of V-Day Toronto, a movement to stop violence against women, and, in 2009, it focused on the DRC. "They realize that the land is occupied and the only way to rid the people is to systematically destroy their families."

This violence is so widespread Médecins Sans Frontières reported 75 per cent of rape victims they treat are in the Democratic Republic of Congo. Physically, the women are often subjected to fistula or HIV. Due to stigmatization, the survivors are shunned by their villages leaving them to deal with the emotional trauma alone.

The result is a population ravished by disease and malnourishment. The UN estimates 1.5 million people are internally displaced and 45,000 die each month.

But it doesn't have to be that way.

By all measures, the Democratic Republic of Congo should be rich. Its fertile land is ideal for growing and minerals are abundant. But, the displaced population puts the agricultural sector in disarray. And, armies control the extraction of minerals by forcing miners to work in deadly conditions for low wages. The armies then sell their plunder to international buyers with annual profits estimated at $144 million.

Lax international laws make it virtually impossible for consumers to determine where the 40 milligrams of tantalum in their cell phone comes from. While giving up the device isn't a viable option in our interconnected world, we can demand transparency.

In Canada, Bill C-300 demands Canadian-headquartered mining, oil and gas companies adhere to the same human rights and environmental standards in developing countries as they do here. Failure would mean loss of diplomatic support, refusal of government loans and stock dismissal from the Canada Pension Plan. The Congo Conflict Minerals Act calls on the United States to cease activities that fund armed groups and contribute to human rights violations.

Support for these laws is needed as is access to information. Consumers can take action on this by demanding companies trace the supply chain and conduct audits that document the routes taken.

The key is not to stay silent.

The key is to let others know, "I'm here."

Bill C-300 passed second reading in the House of Commons and was under consideration by the Standing Committee on Foreign Affairs and International Development at the time of publication. The bill's fate is still uncertain – it passed second reading by only four votes. Both mining associations like PDAC (Prospectors & Developers Association of Canada) and NGOs such as Amnesty International have campaigned on opposite sides of this bill.

Discussion Questions:

1. Often times we are encouraged to check labels on our clothing to see where it comes from. Cell phones we usually don't. Do you know where your cell phone or computer was made? What other products are you unsure of?
2. The conflict in the DRC has been ongoing for many years. Why do you think it receives so little attention in the media? Why do atrocities like the ones described in this column happen with so little intervention?

✳✳✳

Simple solutions can halt cervical cancer
August 31, 2009

A Zimbabwean gynaecologist described to Scott Wittet the smell of a local hospital's cancer ward.

The doctor said he took his interns to visit patients lucky enough to receive treatment or palliative care. As they approached one wing, they were hit by an intense stench. It was overpowering. Many of the interns had to stop, unable to stomach going further.

The gynaecologist explained the source of the odour is more unpleasant than the smell. It comes from a strain of bacteria that finds breeding ground in conditions caused by cervical cancer.

"He told me, I'm not telling you this so you can feel sorry for my interns," says Wittet, who works with the Cervical Cancers Prevention Programs at PATH, a non-profit focusing on global health. "He said, I'm telling you this so you can think about the women dealing with it in their villages."

Cervical cancer is diagnosed in about 500,000 women every year. About 250,000 will die – an estimated 80 per cent of those deaths occurring in the developing world.

But, cervical cancer is largely preventable. It begins with slow-growing, pre-cancerous lesions which can be indentified with screening and removed with cryosurgery, the freezing technique used to remove warts, moles and small skin cancers.

Screening has proven extremely effective. In the United States, the American Cancer Society credits Pap smears, one of the most common methods, with helping to reduce the cervical cancer death rate by 74 per cent between 1955 and 1992.

But, Pap tests remain largely unavailable outside the West.

"It's been so unfair that women in the developing world haven't benefited from screening," explains Wittet. "But, the Pap test is very sophisticated. It hasn't proved sustainable except for in large cities like Bangkok or Kampala."

In low-resource settings, the laboratories that process samples and the accompanied training simply aren't available. Also, results take weeks to be processed. Because women often have to travel hours to reach a clinic, they are rarely able to return for follow-up and treatment.

This means they miss out on early diagnosis and the lesions often progress to cancer. With little access to chemotherapy or radiation, cervical cancer becomes the leading cause of cancer death in women in the developing world.

With limited palliative care, that death can be horrific. The cancer causes tremendous pain. As the odour-causing bacteria manifests, women without access to cancer wards, like the one visited by the Zimbabwean doctor, end up leaving home.

"Not only are they facing their own mortality and tremendous pain, they are facing stigma and loneliness," says Wittet.

But, this doesn't have to be.

There are screening methods more appropriate for low-resource settings. With the political will to fund and train health care workers, they could be made available.

Visual inspection is an easier and faster way to screen. Wittet explains vinegar is used to turn pre-cancerous lesions white. With training, they can be seen with the naked eye. Then, cryosurgery is performed in the same visit to destroy the abnormal cells. Wittet explains freezing is cheap, effective and transferrable to low-resource settings.

In regions where these programs are in effect, the results are promising.

"There are many countries that are building up their visual inspection methods," says Wittet. "Through a five-day training session for local health providers, we create the opportunity to create a cadre of people who can go into the communities."

That's something being desperately sought.

"They've seen this disease in their villages," says Wittet. "This is the disease their aunt, their mom, their grandma died of so painfully."

But, with proper access to screening, that can change. Much of the pain, the loneliness, the loss can be prevented. That is if we take the gynaecologist's advice and start thinking about the women in the villages.

Discussion Questions:
1. How does treatment for illnesses like cancer differ between Canada and Africa?
2. If there are screenings available that would work in low-resource settings, why haven't they been made available on a larger scale? What is holding these programs back?

Multicultural service eases transition into new country, new life, new baby
September 28, 2009

Imagine being admitted to a hospital in a foreign country.

You're alone as doctors explain your condition in another language. On top of that, in just a matter of hours, you'll be completely responsible for a new life.

In one of Vancouver's most multicultural communities, this is exactly what Jalana Grant sees on a regular basis. New parents who are also new to Canada are virtually alone. Some have fled violence while others look to begin a new life. Either way, bringing a baby into that transition is terrifying.

That's where Grant puts her doula skills to work.

Doulas have been gaining popularity but are still relatively uncommon. The word comes from ancient Greek, meaning "woman servant." But, in fact, they are much more.

Doulas are women who provide emotional, physical and informational support before, during and just after childbirth. Unlike midwives, they don't assist in delivery. They help with pain management and act as a coach. They are also a comforter and an advocate in the delivery room.

"Doulas mother the mother and include the partner to make sure everyone is working together," explains Grant, a doula of 26 years. "When labour gets started, the doula comes to the couple's house. As things start to get more interesting, she makes sure they don't end up at the hospital too soon. They are a constant presence so no one has an urgent feeling."

That urgent feeling is hard at the best of times. But, for the women Grant works with as the doula coordinator for the South Community Birth Program, those fears are compounded with other pressing issues.

"We have had women who are HIV-positive, in abusive situations, homeless, single women giving a baby for adoption, concealed pregnancies, teens," says Grant. "Birth is a huge transition and our doulas really make a difference in helping women through this transition, in particular those who are marginalized by class and ethnicity."

As of 2006, about one in five Canadian residents were born outside the country. While a doula's role is usually filled by grandparents, aunts or friends, these people are inaccessible to new immigrants. So is service in a native language.

That's where Grant's team comes in.

The goal is to ensure everyone has a positive birth experience, no matter their circumstance. One client from El Salvador had come to Canada at 14. She lived in foster care and in her twenties became pregnant by a man who was forced to leave the country.

The woman had no family support. But, through her doula, she received care in Spanish. The doula became her mother figure, alleviating the woman's fears and offering encouragement. Afterward she kept the baby, finished her degree at the University of British Columbia and still regularly contacts her doula.

Grant says she often sees women in similar situations and works to pair them with a doula. That means she's always looking to expand her multicultural team.

Recognizing Vancouver's obstetricians can't reflect the city's diversity, Grant seeks women with varied language skills who often don't call themselves doulas but help with pregnancies in their communities.

They are offered official training through DONA International, a doula association providing certification based on international standards, and learn massage techniques and how to determine when to go to the hospital. The volunteers attend a few deliveries as observers. Soon, they begin seeing clients.

Since 2003, they've assisted with over 600 births.

"We speak 17 languages right now as well as English," she says. "But, just when you think you have lots, you have some woman speaking a language you've never heard of."

This makes Grant's search for new doulas a continuing one. As long as there are new moms, she'll need new doulas.

Knowing the answers is easy. Delivering them is the challenge.

Discussion Questions:
1. Imagine you were new to a country and didn't speak the language. What services would you have trouble accessing? What kind of assistance would you need?
2. What are some of the challenges people who have recently arrived in Canada experience when having children?

✳✳✳

Women driving change with a taxi of their own
January 31, 2010

Revathi Roy promises her customers the only thing her drivers will be checking out in the rear-view mirror is the other cars on the road.

That, says the director of Mumbai's For-She Travel and Logistics, is something that can only be guaranteed through a taxi service run by women, for women.

"If a woman looks at you, it really doesn't matter," she says. "There's a level of comfort any time of the day or night."

With over 50,000 taxis traversing Mumbai's crowded streets, very few have women behind the wheel. Roy says women riding alone are often made to feel uncomfortable by ogling drivers who pay them unwanted attention. Further, harassment on public transportation has reached a point where signs have been placed on trains reminding patrons that it's a criminal offense.

That's when Roy came up with the idea of starting a taxi company "as an initiative towards the empowerment of women."

"When we got started, we thought we should do something different. This niche was available in the market," she says. "We have a lot of women, children and young girls."

The first women-only taxi service surfaced in the United Kingdom in 2005. Inspired by its lead, For-She began operations in Mumbai while similar services got off the ground in cities like Moscow, Beirut and Puebla, Mexico.

Some were initiated due to unwanted leering or flirting.

For other cities, the situation was more concerning. In Moscow specifically, the city's cab company was started after reports that a number of women had been assaulted while taking cabs home late at night.

In each of these cities, a women-only cab service is meant to offer comfort that goes beyond seating.

"When the owner of the company visited Thailand, she got the idea because a guide helped her by showing her around the city," says Muriel, the call-center operator for Beirut's Nayaghi Banet Taxi. "The guide was a lady and she felt much more comfortable. Now, we find the customers feel safer, too."

While each service pledges to stand up for women's rights, many say that segregation is really only a band-aid solution. Rather than addressing harassment or violence against women head-on, the burden of protection is placed on women while perpetuating stereotypes that they are defenceless.

On top of this, in countries like Iran where women are already segregated in many facets of society, the women-only taxi service there has been criticized for reinforcing the laws of the oppressive regime.

But, for Roy, For-She is not just about ensuring her customers have a safe ride – it's about empowering her female drivers.

"Driving is my passion," she explains. "It was my love for driving which started everything."

When Roy recruits new women drivers, it's that same love of being behind the wheel of a car that Roy seeks. Through a job at For-She, she hopes this will be a source of economic empowerment.

For-She has now expanded to include a driving school as part of its operations. The women entering the program are trained in motor skills and the rules of the road. As well, they are given classes in first aid and martial arts so that they are "capable of defending themselves and the women passengers in the hour of need."

"First, we look for an ability, an aptitude to drive," says Roy. "Then, we try them out. The course is three months and then they can make 3,000 rupees ($68) per week."

For-She has expanded from Mumbai to include services in New Delhi with proposed projects in Hyderabad, Bangalore and Kolkata.

That way Roy hopes to empower a few more female drivers across the country as well as ensure that more eyes stay on the road and off the passengers.

Discussion Question:
1. Revathi Roy says there is a "niche market" for a women-only taxi service in her city. Is there a similar need in your own city? Why or why not?
2. Some say these taxi services are empowering for women while others say this is a band-aid solution. What is your opinion? Why?

✳✳✳

Skin-tone stigma and the dangers of bleached beauty
March 1, 2010

Mama Apiyo's stall in the Nairobi marketplace is a wealth of beauty secrets. There are balms for styling hair and make-up to cover blemishes.

Then, there are the creams and lotions promising a lighter complexion.

To skeptics, the 35-year-old vendor points to her and her assistant, Ndunge. The women don't just sell, they model. The light-coloured skin on their faces and arms are meant to convince buyers of a "beautiful end product."

Mama Apiyo says, "Both men and women adore and love the after-effects of bleaching which is light and fair skin."

The two women have made a decent living selling the popular brands. But, you don't have to look far to see the true cost of this so-called beauty.

Mama Apiyo has dark blotches around her eyes. Doctors say this irreversible discolouration is the result of overuse. For 30-year-old Ndunge, her skin is more of a translucent yellow. The skin around her eyes even has a tinge of green.

This stall represents an extreme in the quest for this perception of ideal beauty. Yet, bleaching is a cosmetic practice becoming more and more common in countries around the world. For the companies who make the products, the profit is in the billions.

"In Jamaica, it's not abnormal to see people day-to-day who have lightened their skin," says Dr. Neil Persadsingh, a dermatologist in the Caribbean nation. "Most people think it's fine. They associate lighter skin with the opportunity to find a mate or get a job."

In many cultures, lighter skin is often associated with higher privilege. In Asia, actors and actresses with paler skin are usually cast in the more admirable roles. In India, complexion has deep roots in the caste system. There, bleaching products are so widely used that in 2007, commercials featured endorsements by one of Bollywood's top-earning actors and the former Miss World.

In Africa, Mama Apiyo says women, and to a lesser extent men, bleach because of the influences around them. She says advertisements mostly portray light-skinned women who quickly become the envy of people everywhere. Then, she says, women are persuaded by boyfriends and husbands to look more like the advertisements.

"Most times, their men friends admire light-skinned women," says Mama Apiyo. "They feel the pressure to alter their dark-skinned pigment so as to retain their men."

As a result, many put themselves in danger.

Persadsingh says bleaching products work by blocking the production of melanin, a compound that produces skin tone. It also protects against skin cancer. He fears that, on top of short-term side effects like patchy discolouration, glaucoma or stillbirths, users will find increased rates of skin cancer later in life.

Banning the products usually isn't enough as homemade concoctions are already used among the poor. These are often made using hair relaxer, household bleach and other chemicals. The reactions can cause permanent disfigurement from burns.

Still, few heed these warnings.

"After seeing a woman who has flawless skin and have attractive beauty, they wish to be like the model on the advertisement," says Mama Apiyo. "They will go buy the product in spite of being told of the consequences."

That's why stigmas related to darker skin need to change.

This is a process that will take time. It involves breaking down stereotypes built by Western influences and overcoming long-standing traditions, such as the caste system. Although it will be a struggle, it can happen by celebrating positive images of all skin colours.

Government and advertising groups need to lead the way. By ensuring a balance of colours in advertisements and movies, this exposes people to a broader definition of beauty. Hopefully, that will stop people from going to the extremes.

For now, Mama Apiyo continues to woo buyers with neatly-stacked jars of what she calls a beautiful end product. Sadly, her business is booming.

Discussion Questions:
1. To what extent do models in advertisements influence your perceptions of beauty?
2. What things can you do to encourage advertisers to show a broader definition of beauty?

4
HIV/AIDS

When Marc was 18, he deferred his university scholarship to travel to Klong Toey, Thailand to try and make a real difference in the lives of others. After being greeted by the volunteer coordinator and dropping his bags in a small apartment, he was ushered into the AIDS ward of a makeshift hospice.

Of course, it wasn't called an AIDS ward. According to the government at the time, no one in Thailand had HIV/AIDS. Some people got "very sick." Here, it was Marc's job to take care of them.

After a crash course in medicine, Marc was informed he would work the next shift alone. He was terrified at the prospect but did his best to keep the patients comfortable. When a man started to choke, he administered the medicine the nurses recommended. When it had no effect, he got scared.

Marc ran out into the street looking for help. But the passersby refused, afraid of catching AIDS themselves if they entered the ward. His only choice was to sit and hold the man's hand until he died.

This experience in Klong Toey has never left Marc. It was there that his eyes opened to the complexity of the issues surrounding HIV/AIDS worldwide. The stigmas, misconceptions and harsh reality of available medical treatment in the developing world all presented themselves in that tiny hospital.

Since the early 1980s when doctors first recognized Acquired Immune Deficiency Syndrome, or AIDS, and identified the Human Immunodeficiency Virus, HIV, as its cause, millions have been lost in the fight against this disease. It's estimated over 25 million people have died. Every year, the world sees approximately 2.7 million new infections.

Since its discovery, medical advances have taken HIV/AIDS from a death sentence to a chronic, manageable disease. Still, there is no cure. A lack of treatment in the developing world, particularly sub-Saharan Africa, means the epidemic impacts nearly every facet of society.

Despite learning more and more about the virus every day, misconceptions like the ones Marc encountered in Thailand still exist. As he witnessed, they often get in the way of properly treating and preventing the disease.

The following columns were written with the intention of indentifying and correcting a few of these misconceptions. Some, like the story of Glorius Kyarihunda who was murdered after disclosing her HIV-positive status to her husband, bring to light sad and often tragic realities. Others are more hopeful – like Lucy and Emmanuel who continue to have a happy marriage despite Emmanuel being a carrier of the virus.

A cure may still be a long way off. But, it's through education that we can correct these stigmas and hopefully keep more people safe through the course of this struggle.

Distinguishing disease from witchcraft
February 18, 2008

Eunice Kimutai doesn't believe in witches. The trouble is some people in her community do.

A retired school teacher near Tanzania's western border, Kimutai now leads the charge in her village to have people tested for HIV. It's a daunting task, as the elders in her community have taken to telling people who fall ill with the disease that they are possessed by evil spirits.

"When you believe [in] witches, you don't go for a test," says the elderly grandmother. "People say you have to go to a witch doctor instead of going to the hospital."

To counter their claims, Kimutai provides community members with pamphlets on AIDS and encourages those with symptoms of HIV to see a doctor, even though witch doctors are much cheaper than hospitals and have become ingrained in local beliefs.

"When you tell them they have signs of HIV, they say 'no,'" Kimutai explains. "It is very difficult."

Her struggle is the kind that often makes headlines out of central and southern Africa. That's where a mixture of folklore and evangelical Christianity in some communities has spawned a fundamentalist belief in witchcraft and possession by evil spirits, one that's blurring the line between traditional medicine and extreme religion throughout the entire continent.

But assertions by the UN and others about the rampant presence of witchcraft in Africa are often sensationalized. That's because much of what the West calls witchcraft is actually just the use of local remedies, often plant-based formulas, made by traditional community healers – something residents have done for centuries.

In North America the word "witchcraft" conjures up stereotypical images of broom-riding women with green faces. In Africa it often involves herbs and rituals that can actually be beneficial.

After the civil war in Sierra Leone, for example, many former child soldiers were welcomed back into their communities only after an elaborate cleansing ceremony that included fasting, repentance and bathing in local rivers. This was an essential form of social acceptance and forgiveness for the children whose role in the war initially left them outcast.

There are also some extreme cases where evil spirits are blamed for everything from HIV symptoms – like in Kimutai's village – to the death of a community member. These can lead to suspected victims of possession being banished from their community, or in some cases, calls for an exorcism.

Despite the attention these incidences can attract, they are not the norm and certainly not a reflection of traditional healing on the continent, warns a York University professor and expert in African culture.

"There are particular groups in particular regions that practice exorcism," explains Pablo Idahosa, the director of York's African Studies Program. "You can't generalize. It's like saying Canadians practice exorcism when it's actually just a community in Montréal."

Idahosa points to the rise of fundamentalist evangelical Christianity as a driving force behind these severe forms of witchcraft. He also says that impoverished locals sometimes have no choice but to visit witch doctors, as hospitals are just too expensive for them.

"A lot of this has to do with poverty," he explains.

In these extreme cases, well-funded affordable education and health care programs would help dispel myths about evil spirits and deter the use of witch doctors and exorcism. At the same time, they could empower community healers to join the fight against HIV/AIDS by creating localized approaches that combine traditional and modern medicine – exactly what Kimutai wants to see.

Local healers there have been enriching communities for generations and can play a very important role in both modern medicine and social cohesion. Understanding this can go a long way in better appreciating an often misunderstood continent.

Discussion Questions:

1. This column presents the problem of a sensationalized perception of Africa. What contributes to sensationalism? How can they impede the effort to fight HIV/AIDS?

2. What challenges does Eunice Kimutai face in her efforts to inform her community about HIV/AIDS? If you were in her position, what types of strategies would you use?

✱✱✱

Burden of HIV disclosure falls on Uganda's women
July 6, 2009

Glorius Kyarihunda was murdered by her husband at 25-years-old.

The man hacked his wife of 10 years to death with a machete in Western Uganda when she returned home to retrieve her belongings.

Days earlier, Glorius' husband blamed her for his positive HIV test.

According to the Ugandan branch of the International HIV/AIDS Alliance, Glorius was one of five women murdered in 2008 under similar circumstances. Thousands more suffered abuse or eviction. In a survey of just one district by ActionAid Uganda, 100 out of 465 women said they experienced domestic violence as a result of disclosing their status.

Disclosure is not only difficult, it's dangerous. Yet, just months after Glorius' death, Ugandan Parliament is debating a bill that gives a person six weeks after testing positive to tell their partner before the government does.

The N'djamena "model law" created a guideline for criminalizing the willful transmission of HIV. Adopted across West Africa, it attempts to curb infection and empower victims of abuse or rape.

The law contains important measures criminalizing malicious and intentional transmission. But, these cases are rare. In practice, articles like the forced disclosure rule disproportionally criminalize women living in fear of abuse.

Due to antenatal testing, women tend to find out their HIV status before their husbands. This places the burden of disclosure on them and increases the risk of violence or abandonment. Leaving is rarely an option. Existing laws and tradition often deprive women of property and inheritance rights in divorce. Access to credit and salaried employment is also limited.

"Many women cannot disclose their status to their partners because they fear violent assault or being thrown out of the home," said Edwin Cameron, a Justice of the Supreme Court of Appeal of South Africa at the 2008 International AIDS Conference.

On top of this, the rules of predominantly male-dominated societies leave women unable to negotiate condom use or family planning. Many men, like Glorius' husband, hold their wives responsible for infection.

The problems don't stop at disclosure. In Togo, anyone who doesn't use a condom in "all risky sexual relations" is breaking the law while Guinea requires mandatory testing before marriage. In Zimbabwe, a woman was convicted for "deliberately infecting another person." Her lover has never tested positive for the virus.

In Sierra Leone, women can also be criminalized for exposing their infants to HIV.

"Any person who is and is aware of being infected with HIV or is carrying and is aware of carrying HIV antibodies shall not knowingly or recklessly place another person, and in the case of a pregnant women, the fetus, at risk of becoming infected with HIV," says Article 21 of the legislation.

Due to years of civil war, about 70 per cent of Sierra Leone's population is living below the poverty line. That means access to affordable antiretroviral drugs through international aid is essential. But, coverage is remarkably low. A 2007 UN assessment found only 25 per cent of pregnant, HIV-positive women and less than one per cent of exposed infants received treatment. Further, only 26 per cent of people have access to clean drinking water putting infants at risk of contracting HIV through breast milk or deadly, waterborne diseases through formula.

"We must change the social circumstances that will empower those women to say no when they wish to and to insist on protection when they want to," said Cameron.

In the face of this epidemic, anger and fear can inspire drastic action. But, legislation that ignores the realities of gender inequality only worsens the problem by reinforcing the stigma associated with the disease. That's why our focus should be poverty, the domestic violence and the misinformation that causes infection.

"It is a virus," said Cameron. "Not a crime."

At publication, the HIV/AIDS Prevention and Control Bill (2008) was still under consideration by the Uganda government. However, opposition to the bill has grown, picking up support from organizations like Human Rights Watch and the World Health Organization.

Discussion Questions:
1. What are the good intentions behind laws like the one being debated in Ugandan Parliament? Why do officials think it will curb the spread of HIV/AIDS?
2. Some fear that laws like the ones discussed in this column will make others not want to get tested. Why?

✳✳✳

Helping couples cope with single HIV diagnosis
October 5, 2009

When Lucy Emmanuel learned her husband had tested positive for HIV, she cried.

After nine years of marriage, the 32-year-old from Arusha, Tanzania attempted to process her fears. Lucy tested as well. It came back negative but she found little relief. She worried about her own health and that of her two young children.

Mostly, she worried about her marriage.

An opportunistic infection brought Lucy's husband, Emmanuel Ndolimana, to a clinic. It took him three weeks to tell his wife about the positive result. When he broke the news, he made a request – please stay with me, please be OK with it and please help find a way to work through this.

"I put myself in his place," she says. "I thought, 'What if it was me?'"

There is no greater test of the vow "in sickness and in health" than a single, positive HIV test. Yet, discordant couples – where one partner is HIV-positive and the other negative – are prevalent throughout Africa.

Despite the fear of disclosure and the challenges of the disease, through counselling, couples like Lucy and Emmanuel are staying together, staying healthy and making their marriages work.

"We enforce a positive prevention strategy where we prevent them from infecting their partner," says Cayus Mrina, project coordinator for the African Medical and Research Foundation's (AMREF) Counseling Discordant Couples Project in Tanzania. "To be able to have the skills to disclose and bring up the issue of communication with them and other community members, these are the key things."

Due to the stigma associated with HIV, many fear repercussions for disclosure. There is the risk of transmitting the disease to a loved one. There are also the social challenges. Women especially fear being thrown out of the home and ostracized by the community due to male-dominance in the culture.

"Disclosure is especially low when there is no couple counselling," says Dr. Florence Temu, AMREF's Deputy Country Director. "The issue of fear is there."

Despite their nervousness, Lucy and Emmanuel enrolled in AMREF's program.

For most couples involved, it was the woman who was HIV-positive. Pregnancy means women are more likely to get tested. But, Emmanuel was determined to keep Lucy and their marriage healthy.

In their session, the focus was communication. They discussed prevention methods like sustained and proper condom use. At the same time, they talked about antiretroviral drugs and the importance of a nutritious diet.

From there, they learned how to strengthen their marriage and how to accept their new marital status.

"Women are linked into peer support clubs," says Mrina. "For the few men who are HIV-positive, we encourage them to create a forum for discussion at home."

Through the practices they learned, Lucy has been able to

stay HIV-negative. They have found others who share similar challenges. Their community even started a club. Emmanuel serves as its chair and members openly discuss stigma, prevention and health.

Most importantly, the couple says their love for each other has deepened.

"He takes good care of me," says Lucy. "He loves me very much."

The couple still faces challenges. The two have come to accept the positive test result, but others outside their marriage are less tolerant. Emmanuel left his job when he became ill. Now, he is concerned he won't be able to find an employer who will hire an HIV-positive worker.

At the same time, Lucy worries their extended families will start questioning why she hasn't produced any more children.

But, these are all issues Lucy and Emmanuel are slowly addressing with their counselor.

Emmanuel describes his wife as kind and says he appreciates her acceptance of his status. Both say they love each other very much and that their marriage is strong.

Despite the challenges, their vow is to work through them together.

Discussion Questions:

1. For people who are diagnosed with HIV in Canada, how might their experience differ from Lucy and Emmanuel? Think about both health and societal perspectives.

2. In the previous column, we learned about women who feared being kicked out of their homes if they revealed they were HIV-positive. How does Lucy and Emmanuel's experience challenge that perception? What does this teach us about stereotyping?

Tackling the challenge of keeping Africa's blood supply safe

November 30, 2009

Lying on an operating table, a young woman hasn't yet seen her newborn baby.

But, it's not joy she's feeling, it's fear. A hemorrhage is quickly draining her blood, but the hospital has run out of clean blood for a transfusion.

There is one more pack. It tested positive for HIV, however there's a chance the test was wrong. Here in sub-Saharan Africa, it's not uncommon to find errors in both positive and negative results. That's what makes the decision to give this woman a transfusion so difficult.

In the effort to provide as many life-saving transfusions as possible, blood services struggle to reduce reliance on donations from high-risk groups – namely, family and paid donors – and even to ensure that every donation is free of transfusion-transferable infections.

The heads of national blood services in 37 African countries claim that every unit of blood is tested for HIV. However, the World Health Organization estimates that five to 10 per cent of new HIV infections in Africa, 250 to 500 people every day, result from contaminated blood used in life-saving operations.

Blood transfusions are the primary treatment for severe anemia caused by malaria or malnutrition and complications related to childbirth and trauma. Along with HIV/AIDS, these represent the worst health problems facing Africa's people, especially pregnant women and children.

With between 350 and 500 million cases of malaria each year and 14 million cases of birth-related hemorrhage, many people are at risk of contracting HIV, hepatitis or syphilis in the attempt to fight these preventable problems.

WHO data from 2004 shows 87 per cent of African countries collect less than half of the blood they require to meet the needs of their populations. With only 2.8 million units collected in that year for the 720 million people of sub-Saharan Africa – a ratio that is on average 11 times higher in wealthy nations – transfusions are often unavailable.

In 1999, Jeff Busch travelled throughout the continent asking hospital staff whether they tested their blood donations. Many responded that they didn't have the equipment. Subsequent fact-finding trips and fundraisers led Busch to create the Safe Blood for Africa Foundation, which works with health ministries and community leaders to develop national blood services, train professionals and support donor outreach.

The establishment and support of national blood services has contributed to huge gains in blood collection, proper testing and safe distribution. According to Busch, in the past 10 years, the number of countries with a national service jumped from five to 37. The per cent of donated blood tested for all transfusion-transferable infections went from 15 to 60.

These services centralize funding and human resources, allowing for more accurate testing and effective donor outreach. Clean blood can then be distributed to poor and remote populations.

However, increasing blood supplies from voluntary, unpaid donors remains a challenge. WHO Africa Regional Director Luis G. Sambo estimates eight million units of blood are needed annually – five million more than are currently collected.

That's where Safe Blood for Africa's African Club 25 Society comes in. In 15 African nations with over 62,000 members between ages 16 and 25, Club 25 groups gather to socialize in a risk-free atmosphere. Committing to donate blood 25 times in their lives, members learn about HIV-prevention and healthy lifestyle choices, lowering their chances of contracting and spreading the disease.

One member is 23-year-old Ditshebo Kgamanyane. Upon joining Botswana's Club 25, she started using condoms and began spending time at a local youth centre. Kgamanyane donates blood as often as four times a year with the knowledge that it will save lives.

"Now I also educate my friends on the importance of donating blood and on who a blood donor is," she says. "These days I am also encouraged to participate in other village activities towards HIV prevention and the support of those living with AIDS."

Kgamanyane lives HIV-free not just for her own health, but for the health of her country.

Discussion Questions:
1. Why might family and paid donors be considered high-risk groups for collecting blood?
2. What are some of the risks of blood transfusion and collection in Africa? How does this situation differ in Canada?

5

War & Reconciliation

Back when we decided to stop reading the newspaper (this was before we learned of Archbishop Desmond Tutu's "to-do list" theory), the images of violence and war were what really put us over the edge.

In the age of 24-hour television news and minute-by-minute reporting on the Internet, it's impossible not to be surrounded by images of destruction, debris and suffering. All the while, we learned about the amount of money being spent on troop deployment, weapons and sustaining nuclear arsenals large enough to destroy the world many times over. We read statements about war from politicians in all corners of the globe. Sometimes, we even heard about the political cost of their words.

Rarely did we read about a measure that seemed much more important – the human cost.

One of the best measures came from economists Joseph Stiglitz and Linda Bilmes. Five years after the beginning of the Iraq War, they calculated the cost of the invasion, including elements like caring for wounded veterans and the cost of lives lost within Iraq.

The price tag – about $3 trillion – was discouraging. But, at least they put forward a more accurate representation of conflict. Through Global Voices, we tried to call attention to the human cost of a few other conflicts.

There was Kenya, a country that is very close to our hearts. This is home to many people we call friends and still more who we regard as family. It was them we thought of when we turned on the news and saw images of riots erupting in the streets in December 2007. The incumbent president Mwai Kibaki had been declared the winner in the nation's election, but supporters of his opponent claimed electoral manipulation.

As reports surfaced of targeted ethnic violence, we wanted to better understand what was happening on the ground. A few months later, a coalition government was formed and the violence was quelled. A year later, however, we followed up to see how the lingering effects of conflict were still impacting those in the country.

Through other columns appearing in this chapter, we looked at how failure to speak out could affect a population when South Africa's former-president Thabo Mbeki continued to support Zimbabwean president Robert Mugabe despite his human rights abuses. We also looked at how North American consumption habits could in fact fuel a conflict in Colombia. Finally, as pirates attacked ships off the coast of Somalia, we looked at their reasons for taking arms and learned how years of conflict in this region was leading to other forms of banditry on the high seas.

With each of these columns, we tried to keep in mind the human cost of conflict. We hope that after reading through this chapter, you will approach similar stories you will inevitably read in the media with this same mindset.

Then, by continually considering our shared humanity, we hope this will lead to a more peaceful world.

Violence hurts pride of Kenyans
January 14, 2008

The images of violence that have rocked Kenya since its disputed election may have caught the world's attention, but nowhere have they been more shocking than in Kenya itself.

With upwards of 500 people dead and 250,000 displaced, international media reports quickly began comparing the violence in Kenya to the genocide in Rwanda. This has stunned Kenyans, who are taken aback by the light in which their political unrest has been portrayed.

They too are frustrated by the clashes of the past two weeks and are eager for Kenya to return to the bastion of regional stability it has long been – the place that international aid agencies, refugees from other countries and even the office of the United Nations Environment Programme call home.

"No words can express the absence of pride the entire country feels over the scale of violence that has been witnessed," says Peter Ruhiu, a friend of ours in Nairobi. "What the world is seeing is repressed anger by a minority of frustrated citizens who, having felt let down by a flawed electoral process, have turned their anger on perceived enemies."

The national media has led the way in speaking out against the current crisis. A week into the clashes, newspapers across the country took the unprecedented step of publishing front page editorials calling for an immediate return to calm, all under the headline "Save Our Beloved Country." Radio and television stations read their editorials on air.

"No grievance and no cause is worth the innocent blood of Kenyan children," wrote Nairobi's *Business Daily* newspaper. "It is unbelievable foolishness for Kenyans to destroy their economy, their homes and their entire way of life in the name of politics."

Readers have responded. The comments from Kenya's *Daily Nation* newspaper are full of messages from Kenyans at home and abroad who are outraged by the violence.

"I am very bitter and at the same time very disappointed by what is happening in my country," reads one message. "I think right now the most important thing is for Kenyans to heal," reads another.

The grievances that are now playing out in the media are ones that go far beyond tribal animosity. Kenya is largely made up of a young, impoverished population that lacks the opportunities for a decent life. Despite the country's economic prosperity, the streets of Nairobi and other cities are full of idle young men without jobs or money.

Many Kenyans blame the rampant corruption of leaders like former President Daniel arap Moi for their plight. When his successor, Mwai Kibaki, came to power, he represented the possibility of change for Kenya's 15 million poor.

That hope never materialized though as most citizens have yet to benefit from the country's steady economic growth under Kibaki. For some, the idea of yet another rigged election is just too much to bear.

Everyone is losing in this situation. Kenya's poor are being manipulated by politicians who make promises they cannot keep, while the entire population sees their country descend into violence.

But Kenya is not facing genocide. These protests show that Kenyans will no longer tolerate corruption, and that they now see democracy as their right. The world needs to remember that democracy and life opportunity are as much at stake to Kenyans right now as the country's ethnic relations.

Talk of peace and reconciliation must be accompanied by real improvement in the lives of the poor. Rural economic development, education, foreign aid and the international community's support for democracy are what's needed to bring hope back to a country that desperately needs it.

Discussion Questions:
1. If people are feeling "repressed anger" at a "flawed electoral process," are they justified in using violence? Is there ever a time when using violence is defensible?
2. The authors suggest, "Everyone is losing in this situation." Why? What does this level of violence mean for Kenya?

How the Iraq War's $3 trillion cost to U.S. could have been spent

January 21, 2008

In war, things are rarely what they seem.

Back in 2003, in the days leading up to the U.S. invasion of Iraq, the Pentagon adamantly insisted that the war would be a relatively cheap one. Roughly $50 billion is all it would take to rid the world of Saddam Hussein, it said.

We now know this turned out to be the first of many miscalculations. By 2008, the war in Iraq had cost American taxpayers nearly $500 billion, according to the non-partisan U.S.-based research group National Priorities Project. That number is growing every day.

But it's still not even close to the true cost of the war. As the invasion's price tag balloons, economists and analysts are examining the entire financial burden of the Iraq campaign, including indirect expenses that Americans will be paying long after the troops come home.

What they've come up with is staggering. Calculations by Harvard's Linda Bilmes and Nobel Prize winning economist Joseph Stiglitz remain most prominent. They determined that once you factor in things like medical costs for injured troops, higher oil prices and replenishing the military, the war will cost America upwards of $3 trillion. That doesn't include any of the costs incurred by Iraq or America's coalition partners.

"Would the American people have had a different attitude towards going to war had they known the total cost?" Bilmes and Stiglitz wrote in their report. "We might have conducted the war in a manner different from the way we did."

It's hard to comprehend just how much money $3 trillion is. Even Bill Gates, one of the richest people in the world, would marvel at this amount. But once you begin to look at what that money could buy, the worldwide impact of fighting this largely unpopular war becomes clear.

Consider, according to sources like Jeffrey Sachs, the Worldwatch Institute and the United Nations, with that same amount of money the world could:

- Eliminate extreme poverty around the world (cost $135 billion in the first year, rising to $195 billion by 2015)
- Achieve universal literacy (cost $5 billion a year)
- Immunize every child in the world against deadly diseases (cost $1.3 billion a year)
- Ensure developing countries have enough money to fight HIV/AIDS (cost $15 billion per year)

In other words, for a cost of $156.3 billion this year alone – less than a tenth of the total Iraq War budget – we could lift entire countries out of poverty, teach every person in the world to read and write and significantly reduce child mortality while making huge leaps in the battle against HIV/AIDS, saving millions of lives.

Then the remaining money could be put toward the $40 to $60 billion annually the World Bank says is needed to achieve the Millennium Development Goals, established by world leaders in 2000 to tackle everything from gender inequality to environmental sustainability.

The implications of this cannot be underestimated. It means that a better and more just world is within reach, if we are willing to shift our priorities.

If America and other nations were to spend as much on peace as they do on war, that would help root out poverty, hopelessness and anti-Western sentiment that often fuels terrorism – exactly what the Iraq War was supposed to do.

So as candidates spend much of this year vying to be the next U.S. president, what better way to repair the country's image abroad, tarnished by years of war, than by becoming a leader in global development?

It may be too late to turn back the clock on the past and rethink going to war, but it's not too late for the U.S. and other developed countries to invest in the future.

When this column was originally published, Stiglitz and Bilmes estimated the cost of the war to be approximately $2 trillion. Since then, they raised the estimate to $3 trillion – a figure that has been adjusted accordingly. They also estimate the war continues to cost American taxpayers $7 billion per month and point out that oil *prices have increased since the beginning of the Iraq war from $23 a barrel to about $80 at time of publication.*

Discussion Questions:
1. Some people argue that violence or acts of terrorism stem from situations where people live in extreme poverty or where their human rights are denied. Do you agree? What would a shift in spending from war to poverty reduction mean for terrorism?
2. After reading this article, what do you think defines the "cost of war?"

***

Mbeki has chance to help Zimbabwe – and himself
June 16, 2008

A nation once again holds its breath.

As a runoff election approaches, the future of Zimbabwe hangs in the balance. A victory by opposition leader Morgan Tsvangirai means renewed hope for a country torn apart by decades of corruption. Another stolen election by President Robert Mugabe can only lead to more instability and violence.

Most world leaders recognize these stakes, and call for a peaceful transfer of power continually grow louder, only to fall on deaf ears in Harare. But ironically – and unfortunately for Zimbabwe's 12 million people – the one man who may actually convince Mugabe to step down, South African president Thabo Mbeki, is also the only man unwilling to speak up.

Mbeki's allegiance to Mugabe is unwavering, despite the Zimbabwean leader's transformation from liberator to dictator. Their friendship dates back to the 1980s, when a young Mbeki was tasked with improving relations between the African National Congress and Mugabe's ZANU-PF party. (Both fought white rule and won.)

Since then, Mbeki has grown to admire Mugabe, even as he

systematically destroyed Zimbabwe's economy, instilled fear in his citizens, attacked his opponents and alienated himself from the international community.

"There is an immense respect among people who have fought against the struggle – both apartheid and colonialism," explains University of Toronto politics professor Richard Simeon, who has lectured at the University of Cape Town. "Mugabe was highly respected as a freedom fighter."

This mutual respect gives Mbeki political clout in Zimbabwe, something few outsiders have. But instead of using it to push for reform, Mbeki remains complacent to Mugabe's campaigns of political intimidation.

Mbeki's peculiar declaration that "there is no crisis" following Zimbabwe's initial election round in March – even as Mugabe's henchmen filled the streets after Tsvangirai received more votes than the president and a third candidate – raised eyebrows around the world.

"South Africa was the one country that had the opportunity to bring pressure on him," Simeon says of the March election. "[Mugabe] would have reacted to that more than pressure from any other source."

This ongoing support for Mugabe only adds to the missteps that have left the South African leader's reputation in tatters. Mbeki is well known abroad for his absurd declarations that HIV does not cause AIDS and that antiretroviral drugs are poison – this while nearly 1,000 South African citizens die of AIDS every day.

And under Mbeki, South Africa's impressive economic growth has done little to ease poverty as nearly half the country's population earns only seven per cent of its income. Unemployment is at 24 per cent.

This led to an embarrassing electoral defeat for Mbeki in December as his likely successor, Jacob Zuma, was named the new head of the ANC – even as Mbeki remains the country's president.

If Mbeki is going to begin restoring his reputation, Zimbabwe's runoff election is a good place to start.

With ongoing voter intimidation, it may be too late to ensure a fair election, but if he can convince Mugabe to forego any flawed results and step down – or to at least lessen his grip on power –

Mbeki may be able to repair his legacy.

Mbeki's successor, Zuma, is openly critical of Mugabe and there is little chance he will have the same influence in Zimbabwe. The onus is on Mbeki to act and to act now.

South Africa is the region's most developed nation, meaning it has a responsibility to promote democracy. Without that leadership, the people of Zimbabwe will continue to suffer under the despotic rule of Africa's most notorious tyrant.

More post-election turmoil would mean even more refugees pouring into South Africa, as well as continued instability in an area that cannot afford to be unstable any longer.

Mbeki's continent needs him. He has long promoted African solutions to African problems. This is his chance to ensure just that.

During the second round of the 2008 election, Morgan Tsvangirai withdrew from the race due to violence against his supporters and called on the international community to condemn the vote. Due to the influence of Thabo Mbeki, Tsvangirai and Mugabe later reached a power-sharing agreement. In Sept. 2008, only three months after the Zimbabwe election, Mbeki was forced out of office by the African National Council. Jacob Zuma was elected president in May 2009.

Discussion Questions:

1. Do you agree with the premise that democracy can help facilitate human rights? Why or why not?
2. How do Western nations typically show their disapproval for misuse of power of human rights violations? Do you think they can do more?

Women bear scars of Kenya's post-election violence
March 23, 2009

It's been said silence is golden – not here in Nairobi's Kibera slum.

Kibera is Africa's largest slum and home to an estimated one million people. Last year at this time, it was also home to some of the most intense violence following Kenya's disputed presidential elections.

Today, the effects of that violence linger in the sewage-lined streets and tin-roofed shacks. It's loudest in the five buildings that act as CARE International's sexual violence reporting centres.

Established early in 2008, these centres act as safe havens – places where survivors can gather and speak openly about their attacks.

"We went into the urban areas that were highly-affected by post-election violence," says Beatrice Spadacini, a spokeswoman for CARE International in Nairobi. "But as the violence calmed down, that's when the issue of rape started to emerge."

The violence that plunged Kenya into turmoil last year left 1,500 dead and 600,000 displaced. According to the Federation of Women Lawyers in Kenya, it also resulted in an estimated 3,000 rapes.

Over a year later, these women are not only dealing with the physical and emotional damage caused by their perpetrators, they are seeking justice. Even though it's slow coming, they refuse to stay silent.

"Once you have a law in place, that's something you can't take for granted," says Spadacini. "But the implementation of that law and actually prosecuting is a whole different story."

That story began on Dec. 30, 2007, when incumbent President Mwai Kibaki was declared re-elected despite challenges from his opponent, Raila Odinga. Riots erupted in the streets that involved ethnic violence, particularly between the Kikuyu and Luo tribes.

At the Nairobi Women's Hospital, the doctors were overwhelmed. In the first two days of violence, the hospital's chief nurse reported treating 56 assaulted women and children and feared they weren't reaching hundreds of others.

"Immediately after the violence, their medical needs were primary," says Spadacini. "Then there were the legal issues and how to get these women justice."

Kenya's Sexual Offenses Act was passed in 2006. Before this, the law lacked a clear definition of rape or guidelines for sentencing. The new law has been difficult to implement – but the post-election violence provided a particular challenge because of the chaos and sheer number of victims.

CARE went to work establishing reporting centres. Soon, the women began showing up. In all, the centres have collected 300 testimonies – in 60, the reported perpetrators were members of the Kenyan military.

"If they want to file, they can do so confidentially," says Spadacini. "Unfortunately, a lot have been perpetrated by law enforcement agencies so they are afraid."

Unfortunately, a year after the violence, only four men had been brought to trial.

None had been convicted.

Still, the women gather at the reporting centres – that's where Spadacini says their courage comes through despite the impunity. The women provide each other with the emotional assistance and the group gatherings ensure they do not feel isolated. Many have since tested positive for HIV – at the centres, councillors help them with treatment and therapy to deal with their new status.

As well, Spadacini says the women have set up a loan program where they pool their monthly savings and donate it to individual women. This helps each of them rebuild their homes and businesses destroyed during the violence.

Most importantly, it ensures the women do not remain silent.

"I spoke with one woman who was raped and is now HIV-positive," says Spadacini. "She told me, 'I am a Kenyan. I have the right to speak. And I'm going to for the sake of other women so that no one stays silent on these issues.'"

That way, even when justice fails, the women don't.

Discussion Questions:

1. Why do you think the authors chose to revisit this story a year after the violence took place? What's new to the story? What are the long-term implications of the incident?

2. In the column, Spadacini says, "Once you have a law in place, that's something you can't take for granted. But the implementation of that law and actually prosecuting is a whole different story." What is the difference between passing a law and implementing a law? Why is the latter so difficult?

✱✱✱

Fighting drugs by focusing on demand
May 25, 2009

It seemed strange so many people finished their meals at the same time as Colombia's former president César Gaviria.

We sat next to him at a dinner in the Latin American nation when he invited us outside to continue our conversation. We pushed aside our plates and slowly rose.

So did another third of the room.

We walked out discussing Gaviria's role in the War on Drugs. He had fought the powerful Medellin Cartel led by the infamous Pablo Escobar. During his presidential campaign, candidates had a better chance of being assassinated than elected. Gaviria felt that sting personally. His sister was murdered in 2006.

That's when it became clear the people walking among us weren't a coincidence – they were a security escort. That's also when Gaviria explained the drug trade might be Latin America's issue, but it's North America's problem.

From cocaine in Colombia to opium in Afghanistan to marijuana in West Africa, the drug trade is a dangerous world. Since mid-January, we felt this violence in British Columbia's 20 gang-related murders. These incidents are rightly appalling but only a taste of what Latin America and other wartorn nations have experienced for decades.

Gaviria now advises Mexico on dealing with its 10,000 drug-related murders since 2006. That's how he's come to the conclusion the only stability offered in this violent business comes from North American demand.

Our strategy in the War on Drugs has traditionally been to cut off supply. Aircrafts locate coca farms and drop a powerful herbicide on the plants. This successfully kills it and everything else including legal crops like bananas, coffee and other livelihoods of poor, rural farmers.

Despite treating over 130,000 hectares in 2005 alone, the CIA says that growers began to aggressively replant new terrain virtually cancelling out earlier efforts.

It's the steady North American demand that makes this replanting so lucrative. The annual profit for a hectare of coffee, one of Colombia's main exports, is estimated at about $500 while coca will bring in $5,000.

For one young woman, that price difference makes the decision of what to plant a no-brainer.

"The farmers are thinking, 'My kids are starving,'" says Carolina Arcila, a 26-year-old Colombian refugee. "If someone tells you to plant a legal crop and get paid nothing, why would you?"

Unlike students in Canada or the United States, Arcila explained that growing up in Colombia she never saw cocaine in her high school. She did, however, see its effects.

As a teenager, she met returned child soldiers who told her about the brainwashing tactics of the guerrilla armies. She also spoke with individuals who had been kidnapped. One man was tied to a tree for seven months and guarded by a group of soldiers Arcila's age.

Two weeks before her family fled to Canada as refugees, three of Arcila's school-aged friends were kidnapped.

All are atrocities in the name of the drug trade. But, it wasn't until Arcila got to Canada that she actually saw the narcotic.

That's when the bubbly young woman with a seemingly permanent smile got mad.

"Do you understand that when you buy cocaine here, you're giving money to war?" she asked. "It's the same as just handing them a gun."

But guns are exactly the strategy we've taken in the past – and it's the strategy we're currently working with. In April, President Barack Obama's requested $80 million for Black Hawk helicopters to help Mexico fight its growing drug cartels.

As Gaviria stepped into his bullet-proof SUV, that's where his exasperation came out. The man is understandably tired. Tired of watching his people die. Tired of the negative portrayals of his country. Tired of no one taking responsibility for our demand.

That's where the long-term solution lies. He's just tired of waiting.

Discussion Questions:

1. Former Colombian President Gaviria believes that it is North America's responsibility to solve this problem. Do you agree or disagree with his comments?

2. The authors come to the conclusion that the "only stability offered in this violent business comes from North American demand." What is inferred in this argument? What needs to happen to stop North American demand?

✳✳✳

Somali piracy problem extends beyond the reefs
June 22, 2009

Everyone agrees that there are pirates off the coast of Somalia. Actually identifying them is tougher.

To the Western media and commercial shippers, the men riding the outboard motors equipped with AK-47s are the pirates. Their speed – it takes, on average, eight minutes to board a ship – is too quick for even the fastest U.S. warship. The ransom demands impede business for everyone.

But, the men boarding the boats don't see themselves as pirates. As a lawyer defending one man in the Netherlands said, he is a modern-day Robin Hood. Steal from the ships of rich countries to give to their poor families back in wartorn Somalia. For a country in the midst of conflict where 73 per cent of the population lives below the poverty line, Robin Hood is better than starvation.

The Somalis will tell you pirates exist beyond the coral reefs. But, you won't find them on outboard motors with AK-47s. The real pirates, they argue, are the foreign commercial fishing fleets that have plundered the Horn of Africa's valuable fish and devastated the local fisherman.

With all of this finger-pointing on the high seas, distinguishing Robin Hood from Captain Hook can be a difficult task. That's why hearing both sides is so important.

In 1991, Somalia's last functional government collapsed leaving 3,330 kilometres of coastline unguarded – unguarded and rich with seafood.

As the Somali people watched their country descend into chaos, they also watched ships emerge on the horizon. Some dumped toxic waste – so much the tsunami threw it onto beaches causing radiation sickness among the local population. Then came the trawlers from Asia and Europe using underwater lighting to lure their catch away from coastal fishermen. Local business plummeted while the United Nations estimates $300 million worth of seafood is stolen each year.

"Fishing is a brutal business," says Peter Lehr, author of *Violence at Sea: Piracy in the Age of Global Terrorism.* "These trawlers are more powerful than the Somali fisherman and they basically chase them out of the waters."

To the fishermen, these ships are the pirates. With no government to defend them, they took to the seas themselves.

The fishermen formed a "coast guard," teaming up with local militias and warlords to scare off the foreign pirates or demand "taxes." Lehr explains they financed themselves originally through knife-point robberies. Like smart businessmen, they invested.

Using their plunder, the Somali "coastguard" bought more powerful weaponry and GPS locators enabling them to board bigger ships. Bigger ships meant bigger ransoms. The average now stands at about $2 million.

Suddenly, "defending" Somali waters became lucrative business. So much so that some groups began hiring on-shore caterers with Western cooking skills to feed their hostages.

Now, they've begun moving out of Somali waters and into the coast off Oman.

"There are only a few options here," says Lehr. "You can wait for social welfare, you can starve or you can try to do something else to feed your family. In Somalia, that's mostly piracy."

Of course, the motives of the Somali pirates aren't completely altruistic. What started as a form of vigilante defence has become organized crime. They've been known to steal from local fishermen, too. Bigger business means bolder action. In recent months they've travelled out of Somali waters and attacked legal vessels.

But, it's still important to remember there are other criminals in these waters – ones who are equally guilty of plundering. Simply hunting down the men on the outboard motors is only addressing half the problem. The international community needs to start pointing fingers at the other group of pirates – ones that hail from shores closer to our own.

There are two groups of pirates off of the Horn of Africa. We need to bring both of them to justice.

Discussion Questions:
1. What do you imagine when you think about the story of Robin Hood? Do you see any similarities between this character and the Somali pirates? Do you see any differences?
2. The Somali pirates believe there are other pirates in the waters. Do you agree with the characterization that foreigners could also be considered pirates? Why or why not?

yes we can!

6
Barack Obama

Yes, we can.

Three words that, combined, create what is quite possibly the most well-known phrase of the decade. Back in Jan. 2008, then-senator Barack Obama spoke them aloud before a packed auditorium. They chanted the phrase and the whole world seemed to join in as Obama spoke on.

"Yes we can heal this nation. Yes we can repair this world. Yes we can," he said.

If you watch that oration today, it's hard to believe that excited crowd was listening to a concession speech. Obama just had lost the New Hampshire primary to rival Hillary Clinton. Still, many say this was the tipping point when he managed to win over the hearts and dreams of millions.

By August, the defeat was a distant memory as he won the Democratic nomination. It was forgotten the night of Nov. 4, when he walked on stage in Chicago the President-Elect of the United States of America.

But, of all his speeches, there's a reason why "Yes, we can" still stands out. Even in defeat, even in the face of a great challenge, Obama still managed to give people hope. That's a feeling that lives on in spite of the enormous problems facing our world today.

There are some who think hope is overrated – especially given the portfolio Obama inherited. The problems included two wars in the Middle East, a health care system in chaos, the environment slowly deteriorating and the worst financial crisis since the Great Depression.

Hope might seem futile. In reality, without it, we wouldn't stand a chance. It was because of hope that these pressures didn't seem to weigh on anyone's shoulders the day of Obama's inauguration as thousands descended on Washington, D.C.

Hope is and remains a significant factor in facing each of these challenges. It was with this sentiment in mind that each one of the columns appearing in this section was written.

The first speaks to the world opinion of Obama in the days leading up to the election. The second asks Obama to ensure his legacy doesn't end with his status as the first African-American president. From there, you will find the pieces start to challenge his policies from poppy fields in Afghanistan to the prison cells of Guantanamo Bay.

It's Obama himself who inspires these calls for change by his assertion, "Yes we can repair this world." We don't necessarily think Obama can solve every problem in one go. Although, he has made incredible process in a few key areas including passing a health care reform bill in the United States and bringing nations together to discuss a nuclear-free future.

More than those accomplishments combined, he has managed to give us hope that everyone can be part of the dialogue calling for change.

You see, Obama never proclaimed to the world, "Yes, I can." The operative word here is *we*.

What Obama can do, and has successfully done, is give people hope that by voicing their opinions, they will be heard. Then, by joining together in an iconic phrase, they can create global change.

Yes, we can.

The world's got a crush on Obama
August 25, 2008

Wherever Barack Obama goes, the frenzy isn't far behind.

His supporters pack roadways just to see him speak. They rent billboards. They've even named a drink after him.

But, these supporters won't be voting in November. Actually, they don't even live in the United States.

In July, Obama-mania hit Berlin when 200,000 Germans turned out to hear his speech.

Driving along Pat Bay Highway outside Victoria, B.C., a red, white and blue billboard proclaims, "Obama for President."

In Kenya, the birthplace of the Illinois Senator's father, East Africa Breweries offers Senator Keg beer. Kenyans nicknamed the lager "Obama beer," which is as big a hit as the man himself.

Yes, it's not just YouTube moviemakers who love him – it seems the whole world's got a crush on Obama.

Democrats officially nominated Obama as presidential nominee at the Democratic National Convention in Denver. In November, it will be America's turn to decide. Even though the world doesn't have a vote, they've already cast a symbolic one. They're hoping the change Obama speaks of will resonate outside of the U.S.

"Just imagine if on Nov. 5, the world wakes up and the President is a person of colour named Barack Hussein Obama," says Toby Condliffe, the International Vice-Chair of Democrats Abroad. "That's going to make all the difference in the world right there."

People are definitely attracted to the 47-year-old's charismatic personality. His style is compared to JFK and he attracts screaming fans like the Beatles. But, the young senator's calls for diplomacy are attractive to the international community.

Under the Bush Administration, the American image suffered. The Iraq War created a go-it-alone persona and mustered low opinion ratings around the world.

Obama offers a chance to rebuild that image.

"He's a fresh face, he brings a new approach," says Condliffe. "He understands the world community in a different way."

Obama's foreign policy goals are based around promises of

multilateralism and rebuilding alliances. These goals are evident in his platform.

On terrorism, he wants to see stronger support from America's allies. He is also promising to expand diplomatic presence to impoverished countries. On the environment, he has pledged to lead the G8 countries to a solution on climate change.

"We have long believed that nobody in America is interested in our continent anymore," former German president Richard von Weizsaecker told Germany's *Bild* newspaper. "The appearance and the speech of Barack Obama are evidence that this preconception is false."

Despite his international endorsements, at home Obama is still perceived as lacking experience. The latest polls show he's leading John McCain by a small margin, but Americans are still concerned about his limited time in office.

That's where Obama's international trip has shown his ability to handle global policy. By fostering relationships with international leaders, Obama developed his multilateral policy.

In a globalized world, no country lives in a bubble – including the United States. The country imported a record $31.2 billion worth of foreign oil in May. Europe, Asia and the Middle East own millions of dollars in U.S. treasuries, intricately linked to the dollar and the U.S. economy. The ongoing conflicts in Iraq and Afghanistan are examples of what can happen when armies are spread too thin.

America is so big that the actions of its president affect everyone – not just those who voted for him.

Some have joked the international community should cast 50 per cent of the ballots, sharing the vote with Americans. If this happened, it's clear the vote would tip in favour of Barack Obama.

It appears the world has symbolically cast its vote. In November, Americans will have the chance to cast theirs.

Discussion Questions:
1. Why is it joked that the international community should cast 50 per cent of the ballots in the U.S. election? Do you agree?

What kind of reach does the President of the United States have internationally?

2. Why was Barack Obama so popular with the international community? Do you think he would receive the same reception today as he did in Berlin a few years ago?

✱✱✱

Obama's war must be poverty
November 10, 2008

To President Obama,

Our lives are made up of a series of moments – some good and others bad. Then, there are those that are truly remarkable. These are the defining moments in our lives that shape our perspectives and our personal histories.

Mr. President, there is no doubt that Nov. 4 was a defining moment. Not just for you, but for America and the world as well.

It was not that long ago when Martin Luther King, Jr. delivered his now-famous, "I Have a Dream" speech. How far we have come. Certainly, the title of the first African-American president is distinct. This election made history and its magnitude cannot be discounted.

But, Mr. President, we have one request: Please, do not let this be your legacy.

As King said in 1963, "I have a dream that my four little children will one day live in a nation where they will not be judged by the color of their skin, but by the content of their character."

We believe this day has come.

As a candidate, you made repeated calls for change. Americans have put their faith in you. Now, it is time to follow through on those promises.

That, Mr. President, is where you will build your legacy – where you will find your defining moments.

Like those before you, you will have your own set of challenges. Certainly, the ongoing financial crisis will test your abilities as a leader. Franklin D. Roosevelt led America through some of the darkest times with his fireside chats. You too will need to offer the same support.

You will also inherit the wars in Iraq and Afghanistan. We know America and the world are anxious to see resolutions in these areas. This could be an ultimate test of your abilities.

But, while George W. Bush had his War on Terror and Ronald Reagan his War on Drugs, we would like to see you take on a new kind of war – a War on Poverty.

We live in an increasingly connected world. Although the populations outside the United States had no vote in this election, your actions will affect all of us. So, we ask you to make your mark on the world.

Right now, over three billion people live on less than $2.50 a day. Nearly a billion are unable to read a book or sign their name.

In your own country, the Children's Defense Fund estimates 13.3 million children live in poverty costing the nation trillions in lost productivity, poor health and an increased crime rate.

A War on Poverty will be no easy task. But, this is where we hope to see your character.

For too long, we have elected politicians whose own agendas have dominated policy decisions. You spoke of change. This is where we need it.

In 1961, John F. Kennedy announced his goal to put a man on the moon before the end of the decade. He would never see this come to reality. But, his commitment paved the way for the fulfillment of this extraordinary dream.

Your War on Poverty may not be won during your presidency. But, like Kennedy, we are hoping you will lay the foundation to make an investment in the long-term future of your nation and our global community.

Mr. President, it is clear that you are already breaking ground for minority groups in the United States. This is an incredible accomplishment and one for which you should be recognized.

But, you also have a chance to leave your mark in so many other ways. You asked America to vote for change. They did. Now please, be that change and more.

Discussion Questions:
1. To what extent do you believe Barack Obama is paving the road for minority groups in the United States and Canada?
2. What do you want your legacy to be? What do you want to be remembered for?

✳✳✳

Obama offers new hope on Cuba
January 5, 2009

The United States sure knows how to hold a grudge.

It's been nearly half a century since the United States imposed an embargo on Cuba. The Cold War has long ended, and now even Fidel Castro is fading into the background, but the embargo remains.

You won't find many people outside the United States that support it – the United Nations has condemned the embargo as a violation of international law since the 1990s – but the U.S. has remained resolute. President Bush even enacted changes to bolster the economic sanctions in 2004.

But there is reason for optimism, at last.

Obama has pledged to ease the long-failed Cuba policy. Throughout his campaign, he vowed to make it easier for Cuban-Americans to visit their relatives and increase the amount of money they're allowed to send home to their families.

After changes by the Bush administration, Cubans living in the United States are only allowed to visit the island once every three years, and can send back a maximum of $300 per household, quarterly, to immediate family members.

Since the election in November, pressure has been mounting for Obama to go even further than his initial promises. The leaders of 14 Caribbean nations called on Obama to lift the embargo at a summit in early December and even American businesses have had enough.

In a letter to the President, business associations including the American Farm Bureau Federation, Business Roundtable,

National Retail Federation and the U.S. Chamber of Commerce, made their case for open trade with Cuba.

"Your administration has a unique opportunity to take steps to end nearly 50 years of isolation from Cuba and the Cuban people," they said. "We support the complete removal of all trade and travel restrictions on Cuba. We recognize that change may not come all at once, but it must start somewhere, and it must begin soon."

While the embargo has failed to bring about democracy in Cuba, its effects have been dramatic. Food shortages and a lack of clean water and medicine can all be at least partially blamed on the stubborn American policy. Add on a series of devastating hurricanes, and it's clear that the people of Cuba need help more than ever.

And there's another advantage to lifting the embargo. As Mark Falcoff, an expert on Cuba and author of *Cuba the Morning After: Confronting Castro's Legacy*, explains, without America as an enemy, the Cuban government would have no one to blame.

"The main argument for changing U.S. policy is that it shifts the onus of why there has been no improvement in political freedom in Cuba onto the Cuban government," he says. "In effect, it robs them of using America as an excuse."

It seems unlikely that Obama will go as far as to eradicate the embargo, but some changes are on the way. Beyond the remittances and travel for Cuban-Americans, it's certainly possible that Obama will remove Cuba from the list of terrorist-sponsoring states and might even remove the travel ban.

Any or all of these would be steps in the right direction, but as Falcoff points out, for Cuba to move forward, it's important to remember that change must come from Havana too.

"What the U.S. does or doesn't do is not going to determine the outcome in Cuba," he says.

When President Barack Obama takes office, it will undoubtedly usher in a new era in Cuban-American relations. But whether or not it leads to a better Cuba is up to them.

Soon after this article's original publication, Obama lifted restrictions on the duration and frequency of Cuban-American families visiting the country. He also increased the amount of money

U.S.-based families can send their relatives. Cuba still remains on America's list of terrorist-sponsoring states alongside countries like Iran, Sudan and Syria. Obama has continually stressed that any further progress in U.S.-Cuba relations is reliant on Cuba making moves toward democracy. In Sept. 2009, Obama extended the embargo by one year while the United Nations General Assembly condemned the measure for the 18th time.

Discussion Questions:
1. In this column, the authors refer to America's Cuba policy as "long-failed." Why hasn't the embargo worked in bringing democracy to Cuba?
2. What would improved relations mean economically for the United States? For Cuba?

✳✳✳

Take inspiration from historic moment
January 19, 2009

We're a little jealous of those who will be lining Pennsylvania Avenue on Jan. 20.

Anyone able to snag a coveted spot along the procession route will truly be witnessing a moment of history. We, like millions of others around the world, will be watching the historic moment on television.

Then, the world will take a collective breath as Barack Obama places his hand on the bible and recites the oath that no African-American has ever recited before.

"I do solemnly swear that I will faithfully execute the office of President of the United States, and will to the best of my ability, preserve, protect and defend the Constitution of the United States."

As the scene unfolds, we are sure to see the same tears of joy that marked his acceptance speech back in November. But in those tears, we see not a happy ending. Rather, we see a new beginning, a new way forward and the realization that momentous change can happen in one person's lifetime.

"More than anything, Obama's achievement as a black man in America represents the hope that historical injustices can be overcome," says Jonathan White, professor of sociology and political economy at Bridgewater State College. "Obama's election ultimately represents hope for a more humanistic and sane world order."

One of the most incredible aspects of this progress is how quickly it has come. So often we hear that real transformation takes generations – that it is idealistic to think that we can change the world in our lifetimes.

Tomorrow will stand as a day that proves this is simply not true.

This is because our history is a relatively short one. When we think about it, it was only 202 years ago that the British Parliament officially banned the slave trade. It was only 144 years ago that the Thirteen Amendment was added to the American constitution, abolishing slavery.

Then, there are the events that happened within recent memory – events that our parents and grandparents saw with their own eyes. In 1955, Rosa Parks famously refused to give up her seat on a bus in Montgomery, Alabama. Oprah Winfrey – who had her dress for inauguration day picked out in November – was a year old at that time.

In 1968, Martin Luther King, Jr. was assassinated on the balcony of a Memphis hotel fighting for the cause he believed in. Rev. Jesse Jackson was there that day. Tomorrow, he will stand amongst the crowd watching as Obama is sworn in as President.

Tomorrow, we will witness what most never thought possible in their lifetimes. Hopefully, it will get young people excited about what they might see in their lifetimes.

"It's now up to us to utilize this historical moment to create a future," says White. "It reminds us that we must work feverishly and with great determination to help human beings to realize their human rights."

Today the United States celebrates Martin Luther King, Jr. Day. It's a time for all of us to remember and reflect on the not-so-distant past. Tomorrow, Obama will be sworn in as president, a symbol of just how far we have come.

Knowing this, we can start working towards the progress that could – and should – be seen in the lifetimes of the next generation.

It has been only 44 years that the Voting Rights Act banned practices responsible for the disenfranchisement of African-Americans. If, less than half a century later, that same country can make such incredible progress, imagine what we can do in the next half century on poverty, genocide and environmental degradation.

Progress is possible and tomorrow's ceremony is proof. It's up to us to make sure that progress continues.

Discussion Questions:
1. Why is the election of an African-American president so significant at this point in history?
2. As this column points out, Obama represents some incredible progress for African-Americans in the United States. What other movements do you predict will progress in your lifetime?

✹✹✹

Legal poppies a prescription for Afghanistan
April 20, 2009

In Canada, poppies are already associated with war – or at least with remembering those that died in service. But this little red wildflower has a much bigger role in the ongoing conflict in Afghanistan.

The Taliban insurgency is fuelled almost entirely by flower power.

Afghanistan produces 93 per cent of the world's opium, and 80 per cent of its heroin, both products of the poppy seed. Most of the money made from this illegal drug trade is funneled into the Taliban and used to purchase weapons and train new members.

In his new plan for Afghanistan, President Obama has pledged more troops and a greater focus on development, but he still favours the destruction of poppy fields. At a forum in Brussels last month, Richard Holbrooke, America's top envoy to Afghanistan, called this practice "wasteful and ineffective."

By destroying their only means of income – the illegal drug trade accounts for over half the country's GDP – Holbrooke said that the eradication of poppy fields is "...pushing farmers into the Taliban's hands."

A year earlier in a column in the *Washington Post*, Holbrooke went as far to say that poppy field eradication "...may be the single most ineffective program in the history of American foreign policy. It's not just a waste of money. It actually strengthens the Taliban and al-Qaeda."

Ridding a country of its primary source of income isn't a sustainable option, but cutting off the Taliban's funding and quelling an illegal drug trade are important goals.

The Senlis Council, an international drug policy advisory forum, has proposed a solution that is gaining some momentum: legalize it.

No, we're not advocating the legalization of opium or heroin, but legalizing the poppy agriculture in Afghanistan with contracts to use the opiates to create medicine, like morphine and codeine.

A 2005 study from the International Narcotics Control Board showed that developing nations, representing 80 per cent of the world's population, consumed only six per cent of the world's morphine supply.

Opiate-based pain killers are already available and cheap, but many under-privileged countries import little or none, largely because they fear the drug will lead to addiction and abuse. Meanwhile, their sick suffer needlessly.

While these drugs can be highly addictive when used illegally, doctors in the western world have had great success in treating patients with opiates, and report low levels of addiction. With an aggressive education campaign on the benefits and realities of opiate-based pain killers, developing nations could cause an enormous swell to the world's demand for poppies.

Those suffering from severe or chronic pain could finally get some relief, and the farmers of Afghanistan would have a legal market for their crops.

Of course, a legal poppy trade is no panacea for the problems facing Afghanistan. Removing the Taliban's primary source of income would be a major blow, but it must be only one element to a holistic solution.

Military operations will undoubtedly need to continue for the foreseeable future, but they must coincide with reconstruction efforts to build the infrastructure necessary for the country to enter the modern era.

And while undermining the criminal element that runs the opium trade will help stabilize the country, a strong international presence will be required to guide Afghanistan towards a stronger democracy.

Earlier this year, Stephen Harper told CNN's Fareed Zakaria, "Quite frankly, we are not ever going to defeat the insurgency."

That, of course, depends on how you define a win in Afghanistan.

Harper is correct; quite likely there will always be at least a small fraction of people fighting there. But by cutting off the Taliban's funding, and slowly shifting our focus from military action to stabilization and reconstruction efforts, there is every reason to believe that Afghanistan can grow as a healthy democracy.

And that, we'd call a win.

Obama has since reversed the military's eradication approach to the opium harvest. A $300 million dollar program now distributes grants to Afghan food-processing and food-storage businesses and sells fruit seed and livestock to farmers at a discounted price causing opium production to drop by 22 per cent. The U.S. plans to continue expanding this program and offer more legal crop alternatives to Afghan farmers in the coming year.

Discussion Questions:
1. What would be your initial reaction to legalization of poppy agriculture? Do you think the destruction of poppy fields could strengthen the Taliban or al-Qaeda as Holbrooke suggests? Why or why not?
2. What is your definition of "winning the war?"

Obama yet to live up
to human rights pledge
January 4, 2010

U.S. President Barack Obama had a good first day on the job.

Within 24 hours of his inauguration, he signed orders that banned torture, closed black prisons run by the CIA and called for the closure of Guantanamo Bay by January 2010. With the stroke of a pen, the new President turned his back on some of the Bush-era's most offensive policies

That was day one. As we approach day 365, the President has admitted he won't meet Gitmo's January deadline.

That's not really the concern. As Democratic Rep. John Murtha put it, "The problem with Guantanamo was never about the bricks and mortar. The problem with Guantanamo is that its very existence stains and defies the moral fiber of our great nation."

Rather than the building itself, it's what went on inside Guantanamo that was so offensive. As allegations of torture, abuse and lack of access to international law come out of the Bagram Theatre Internment Facility, a detention centre in Afghanistan, it's clear the issue isn't closing Guantanamo Bay. It's guaranteeing human rights.

The Bagram detention centre lies in a secret location north of Kabul and is currently estimated to hold 600 prisoners – three times that of Guantanamo – without charge. Bagram was not included under a 2004 Supreme Court decision that extended habeas corpus, the right to challenge detention, to Guantanamo. Now, there is evidence that a number of prisoners are in need of that contest.

The United States contends because the prison is in a battle zone, it's not possible to conduct investigations into individual cases. That means prisoners lack access to lawyers.

But recently, two teenaged Afghan boys told the *Washington Post* that this year in Bagram "they were beaten by American guards, photographed naked, deprived of sleep and held in solitary confinement for at least two weeks," clear violation of Obama's torture ban. Further, former detainees told the *New York Times* that some prisoners are kept hidden from the Red Cross, the only civilian organization allowed access to the centre.

These are not the only allegations of misconduct. The British government recently revealed that two men were captured in Iraq in 2004, transferred to Afghanistan by the Americans and have been held in Bagram ever since. Reprieve, a London-based legal charity, has identified the men as Amanatullah Ali and "Salahuddin," and says this transfer amounts to extraordinary rendition, a violation of international law.

Through investigations, Reprieve says it found that Ali may have been captured mistakenly. He is being held as a member of a Sunni extremist group when in fact he is a Shia Muslim. Reprieve also says the other man is said to be in "catastrophic mental and physical shape" due to torture he has suffered since arriving in Bagram.

Still the detention centre is shrouded in secrecy. The exact number of prisoners it holds is an official secret. Obama rarely mentions its existence. Journalists and lawyers are banned from the premises.

In response to allegations of abuse, the Pentagon stated simply, "[U.S.] Department of Defense policy is and always has been to treat detainees humanely."

This isn't the kind of transparency Obama promised on his first day.

As the President told Congress in February, "There is no force in the world more powerful than the example of America... Living our values doesn't make us weaker, it makes us safer and it makes us stronger."

These are fine words, but ones Obama must act on. If the allegations of abuse at Bagram are true, Obama must clearly distinguish between state-sanctioned torture and individual actions. Further, they must bring perpetrators to justice.

Without doing so, Obama's efforts to eliminate abuse at Guantanamo are only superficial if they are not applied to Bagram.

Bagram continues to deny its inmates formal trial. However, improvements are reportedly on the way. The U.S. is planning to open a new detention facility in Afghanistan with larger cells, up-to-date medical equipment and rooms for vocational training. The official date for closing Guantanamo Bay is still yet to be announced. At publication, the U.S. government planned to repatriate 150 prisoners to their respective countries, excluding 50 inmates deemed too dangerous to release or too difficult to prosecute.

Discussion Questions:

1. Obama's very first order as President was to call for the closure of Guantanamo Bay. What did this move signal about his priorities? How did this separate him from the former president, George W. Bush?
2. If Guantanamo Bay closes but Bagram remains operational, do you think this is a victory for human rights? Why or why not?

7

The Economy

In the last chapter, we talked about the enormous challenges on U.S. President Barack Obama's plate. The economy – or more specifically the financial crisis – is probably one of the biggest.

This massive system details our interactions with money, jobs and wealth. Yet, it's not something with which we can easily connect despite the fact that it touches our lives every single day. For many, falling stock charts and suits on Wall Street simply don't relate.

Earlier, we spoke of the human cost of conflict. Over the years, Global Voices has also tried to bring a human voice to the economy. Rather than attempting to explain charts, we tried to explain what they mean to a mother in Ecuador, a working-class family in Cleveland or an investor in Baghdad.

The 2007 food crisis is probably the best place to explain that connection – it was certainly an eye-opener for us. Later, you will read about a woman named Andrea Daquilema who was concerned that the rising price of food would cause her to pull her youngest child from school.

Through Andrea, we saw firsthand the impact the economy was having. In one part of the world, a drought had caused crops to fail. That meant there was less food for the same amount of mouths to feed. The remaining food was sold to those who could pay the most to buy it. That caused prices to rise.

At the same time oil was becoming more expensive. Farmers have to use oil to run their tractors and transport food to markets. When the price of oil went up, it cost more to produce these goods. That meant they needed to start charging more.

These are just two of the reasons why food became so expensive for Andrea. She wasn't the only one worrying. In some countries, people protested. In others they rioted.

Today, the price of food has gone back down and the unrest has been quelled. But, it's the falling prices that have created an impact we can feel here in North America.

In the fall of 2008, we suddenly saw the collapse of a number of banks in the United States. Markets like the New York Stock Exchange and the Toronto Stock Exchange nosedived. Then, on Dec. 1, 2008 the National Bureau of Economic Research stated that the United States had officially been in a recession for a year.

Immediately, people started asking why. We quickly learned that for years, lenders had been giving out subprime mortgages, causing the American housing market to boom. In order to make more loans (and make more money through fees), the local banks would take individual loans, bundle them and sell to large Wall Street firms. This meant the local banks weren't responsible for the loans while the larger firms bundled them with other financial services and resold them to investors. This happened so often that those buying and selling often weren't fully aware of what they owned.

But, subprime mortgages were largely given to people who couldn't afford them. They were given adjustable interest rates that in the beginning were low. When they moved higher, many couldn't continue making payments on their homes. When this happened, they were foreclosed. The bank took over the houses and tried to sell them. But, there were so few people looking to buy that prices dropped. Banks, investors and especially ordinary citizens lost large sums of money.

Many couldn't help but wonder if this could have been prevented if only lenders had better assessed a family's income rather than trying to make a sale. That's a question we have asked a few times in Global Voices. If we looked at different measures of the economy – ones that include the human costs – then maybe we would all be better off.

Throughout this chapter, we hope that by reading the human angle of business stories, we can broaden our understanding of the economy. We hope that you can see your place within the charts.

❋❋❋

Asian investment has done little to boost Africa's fortunes
September 24, 2007

Walking along the streets of Khartoum, it's not difficult to find a dim sum restaurant.

It's an odd image, to be sure. The colourful writing of Chinese signs – for everything from restaurants to pharmacies – stand out among the country's dusty capital.

But it's a reflection of Africa's rising economic reality. Foreign investment, once scared away by fears of war, corruption and instability, is pouring into the continent like never before.

In 2006 alone, nearly $40 billion worth of foreign direct investment landed on African soil – more than double the amount in 2004. With a two year increase like that, Africa's growth rate far outpaced both Japan and the United States.

And Asian investors are leading the way. Exploding economies in places like China, India and Singapore mean that those countries are in need of untapped natural resources and fresh markets for their goods. Africa is the perfect fit.

In fact, the economic ties between the two continents are now the strongest in the developing world. China has companies operating in nearly every African country and upwards of 750,000 Chinese nationals work on the continent.

At the World Economic Forum meetings in Dalian, China, the country's political and economic leaders were clearly thrilled to have Africa fuelling their massive economic growth.

But despite the multi-million dollar contracts and trade deals, this new era of cooperation, as the United Nations calls it, has done little to boost the fortunes of Africa.

That's because much of the foreign investment has been geared towards the continent's resource-rich oil and mining industries, which often generate low tax revenues – meaning that little money actually trickles back into the economy.

For example, according to a UN report, Ghana has seen a significant spike in investment into its gold industry, yet receives as little as five per cent of the value for the gold it exports.

So despite its mineral wealth, nearly 80 per cent of the country lives on less than $2 a day.

At the same time, many of the business deals with countries like China are becoming wrapped up in the continent's political troubles.

Beijing has long been criticized for propping up the regime in Sudan accused of committing genocide in Darfur. Nearly two-thirds of Sudan's oil exports are sold to China, in deals estimated to be worth $2 billion.

For the Sudanese government, increasingly isolated for its role in the killing of civilians, that is much needed cash.

While most Western countries would hesitate to work with governments suspected of massive human rights violations, China sees the allegations against Sudan as internal affairs not to be meddled with. For them, business and politics don't mix.

That has many people worried. Bill Richardson, the Governor of New Mexico who ran as a Democratic candidate in the 2008 presidential election, suggested boycotting the Olympic Games in Beijing – something called the "Genocide Olympics" by activists – if China does not do more to end the bloodshed in Darfur.

So if Africa is going to reap the benefits of economic investment, foreign businesses will need to stop treating the continent as a place to flood markets with cheap goods in exchange for oil and minerals, no questions asked.

Thanks to years of structural adjustment by the World Bank and International Monetary Fund, many of the continent's economies are driven by single commodities. Those economies must be allowed to diversify if they are going to compete.

And, Africa itself will have to better attract foreigners to its manufacturing and agricultural sectors alongside its lucrative yet easily exportable natural resources, by clamping down on corruption, red tape and poor governance.

Doing so would mean the billions of dollars pouring into the continent would benefit local populations the way it is supposed to.

That's an investment worth making.

Trade between China and Africa continues to grow, rising to nearly $107 billion (U.S.) in 2008. China's foreign direct investment in Africa reached $5.4 billion (U.S.) in 2008. During the first half of 2009, China's investment in the continent's non-financial sectors (mining, manufacturing, agriculture and infrastructure) grew by 78.6 per cent to $875 million (U.S.).

Discussion Questions:
1. Why are Africa's natural resources so attractive to markets in Asia? What makes this industry so easily exploitable?
2. Do you agree with Bill Richardson's suggestion that we should have boycotted the Olympic Games in China? Why or why not? Do you think a boycott would have made China reassess its influence in Sudan?

***

World food crisis hinders war on poverty
June 2, 2008

It's been a hard year for Andrea Daquilema.

As a single mother of four living in a small community in the Chimborazo province of Ecuador, she's become accustomed to hard times. But the rapidly rising price of food is making it difficult to keep her family fed.

She values education, telling us of her dream for her children to graduate and get good jobs to help the community. But without any attempt to mask her disappointment, she admits that three have already been forced to leave school and go to work.

She worries that if the food crisis continues much longer, her youngest won't be far behind.

All around the world, families are making similar sacrifices. An estimated 100 million people have fallen into poverty over the last two years, as a worldwide food crisis washes out the progress made in the fight against global poverty.

"This is not just about meals forgone today or about increasing social unrest. It is about lost learning potential for children and adults in the future, stunted intellectual and physical growth," said World Bank president Robert Zoellick at a press conference earlier this year. "Even more, we estimate that the effect of this food crisis on poverty reduction worldwide is on the order of seven lost years."

In North America, people spend roughly 10 to 20 per cent of their income on food. To us, the higher grocery bills come as a minor annoyance. But in the developing world, where food already accounts for as much as 80 per cent of their budget, the repercussions are dire.

Families are taking drastic measures to provide temporary relief. They start by pulling their children out of school and putting them to work. Then they stop visiting health clinics in an effort to save money. Finally they sell-off their assets; first their livestock, and then their ploughs and other farming tools.

Arif Husain, Programme Advisor for the United Nations World Food Programme (WFP), explained how this exacerbates the problem.

"This really puts them into economic destitution, so even when things come back to normal, they cannot remain productive members of society," he said.

The WFP feeds 73 million people in 78 countries, but higher food prices are threatening many of their projects.

For some children, the organization's school feeding programs provide their only meal of the day. But the WFP has already suspended that service to 450,000 children in Cambodia and warns they face similar difficult choices in many more countries.

In March, the organization asked governments for an additional $500 million (U.S.) on top of its normal budget for 2008. Since then, revised estimates show a shortfall of $755 million.

Emergency funding is urgently needed to keep projects like school feeding afloat and to keep people from going hungry. But as Mr. Husain points out, long-term initiatives are the key to ending the crisis.

"You have to ensure that there is investment in the agricultural sector. You have to ensure that agricultural productivity is increasing. These things need to be started now, so that in five years we will see progress. But if we don't start now, this thing will continue."

Andrea Daquilema's three oldest children have started to adjust to life outside school. They take pride in helping their mother and keeping the family fed.

But in her youngest child lies a world of opportunities: a good education, a good job and the chance to break the cycle of poverty.

The global food crisis poses an immediate threat to millions of people around the world, and to a mother's dream for a better future.

Discussion Questions:
1. How do oil prices affect the price of food? How far does your food travel before you eat it?
2. What are some of the pros and cons of delivering food aid in emergency situations? Is it sustainable?

✳✳✳

Making homes affordable in Mumbai
June 23, 2008

The narrow streets weaving through the slums of Mumbai are lined by rows on rows of corrugated tin shacks. Most of them rusted and seemingly on the verge of collapse.

Outside, upwards of a million other people too poor even for a shack live among piles of garbage. There are so many that the sidewalks are nearly impassable.

They exist in the shadows of Mumbai's apartment buildings – some glitzy enough to rival the famous addresses of Manhattan both in luxury and price. Others are more run-of-the-mill but still cost thousands of dollars a month just to rent.

Such is life in India's financial capital where skyrocketing real estate prices have created two worlds in this city of 14 million people. Space now goes for a premium there as villagers continue to pour into a city that struggles to fit them all, making Mumbai among the most expensive places in the world to live.

But many in the city remain desperately poor, unable to afford a decent place to call home. Half the city's population still lives in slums without proper access to water, health care and sanitation. They continue to live in squalor, untouched by India's economic success.

Housing prices there are usually directly quoted by size and can range anywhere from $25 to $2,000 per square foot. Even the most basic accommodation costs around $15,000. That's a hefty price tag in a country where 42 per cent of the population is living on less than $1.25 a day in 2007.

Despite this widespread poverty, huge real estate deals continue to make headlines. In May, Bollywood star Vinod Khanna set a national record by purchasing a three-bedroom apartment in South Mumbai for a staggering $25,000 per square foot. In other words, each floor tile cost him more than a mid-sized car.

Even the national government, which usually downplays India's economic disparity, acknowledges the housing shortfall and admits the entire country is in need of 25 million more homes. The Ministry of Housing and Urban Poverty has vowed to act, but progress remains slow.

That is why the private sector is stepping up. The Monitor Group, a global management consulting firm, is leading the push for affordable housing. They've discovered that, even with Mumbai's real estate boom, inexpensive housing can still be made appealing for investors – if done properly.

"We started looking at development and realized there is an opportunity for market-based solutions for social change," explains Ashish Karamchandani, CEO of Monitor's India office.

Banks and developers have long been wary of investing in low-income housing, worried they would not be able to sell many units. But by encouraging Indian companies to allow stable payroll deductions from their employees, while helping to finance loans through microcredit institutions, Monitor has found a way to ensure that even much of the city's poor can afford to buy a property.

"That fundamentally changed the economics," Karamchandani says.

And it's already paying off. Residents are thrilled about buying an apartment and plans are in the works for two housing units in Mumbai, as well as one in Western India.

Monitor's approach is one that others can learn from. From Rio to Shanghai, developing cities around the world lack affordable housing. Rural residents continue to pour into urban areas looking for jobs, only to find themselves without adequate shelter.

In China alone, 13 million people migrate to cities each year. Without proper housing, poverty becomes inevitable for them.

But as Karamchandani explains, financing is only the first step. Growing urban populations also need adequate services such as transportation and education to ensure sustainable living. Monitor is working to provide Mumbai's poor with just that.

"If you want to play in this field," he says, "you need to develop end-to-end solutions."

Discussion Questions:
1. This column suggests a major divide between the rich and the poor in India. What do you think about this gap? Do you think it's fair that some people live in shacks while others can afford such expensive accommodation? Is the gap between the rich and poor in Canada fair?
2. What are some of the services that go into making a community run? How does a lack of services like running water or sanitation perpetuate poverty?

✳✳✳

Money ties China, U.S. together
July 14, 2008

Money makes for strange bedfellows.

As many countries consider boycotts, George W. Bush confirmed that he would attend the opening ceremonies for the 2008 Beijing Olympics.

Less than 20 years since tanks rolled through Tiananmen Square, China remains a hotbed of human rights abuse and environmental degradation. But the United States has been cautious with its criticism of the emerging superpower.

The reason is largely financial.

The economic ties between China and the United States run deep. China relies on the United States as their largest export market, just as the United States relies on China to fuel its outrageous consumption with cheap imports.

"It's kind of like the relationship between a junky and a dealer," explains economics expert Nicholas R. Lardy of the Peterson Institute. "The junky needs the dealer so he can get his fix, but the dealer also needs the junky to buy his drugs."

Trade between the two nations is rising at a dizzying pace. In 1980 their trade totalled $5 billion. Last year it was $387 billion. It is also heavily lopsided.

The U.S. imports far more from China than it exports, resulting in a trade deficit of over $250 billion. This enormous consumption is rapidly pushing America's debt towards $10 trillion.

The numbers can get overwhelming and the question becomes: how does America stay afloat?

The U.S. economy is buoyed by foreign investment into its treasury securities. Japan still possesses the largest holdings, but China is catching up. Since 2000, China's ownership of U.S. securities has grown from about $50 billion to over $500 billion.

Some political pundits are concerned that by becoming America's banker, China could exercise significant influence over the United States. But that's not really the case.

There's an old adage that says, if you owe the bank $100, that's your problem. If you owe the bank $100 million, that's the bank's problem.

China is now so deeply invested in U.S. securities that any disruption to the value of the dollar would be a serious blow to their own reserves. And since they rely on the U.S. market for their exports, they're forced to buy up new securities as soon as they're issued to prevent the yuan from appreciating against the dollar.

Neither country holds a significant advantage over the other. Despite the enormity of the U.S. economy, the two nations have built a system of co-dependency. Or as Catherine Mann, professor of economics at Brandeis University and former adviser to the chief economist at the World Bank puts it – a system of Mutually Assured Destruction.

"I think you can characterize it a lot like nuclear weapons," she says. "Whoever uses the weapon, invariably gets hurt too."

Each country has the means to significantly disrupt the other's economy, but the collateral damage within their own country could be just as severe.

In short, the United States needs China for cheap imports and foreign investment. China needs the American dollar to remain strong to preserve the value of their foreign reserves and to keep the price of their exports appealing.

This co-dependency is perhaps the reason why the United States has remained relatively quiet while China continues its oppressive policy towards Tibet, suppresses freedom of speech and erodes the environment.

It should be noted that China has made progress over the last 20 years, but there is still much work to be done. As the Olympics approach, the protests and boycotts will escalate. But as the voice of the international community rises, don't expect more than a whisper out of the United States.

They say "money talks," but sometimes it knows when to keep its mouth shut.

Bush ultimately did attend the Beijing Olympics opening ceremonies amidst protests in countries around the world. In Beijing, Reporters without Borders pirated a radio frequency and broadcast criticism of China in Mandarin, French and English for 20 minutes on the day of the opening ceremonies.

Discussion Questions:
1. What is co-dependency? How does the relationship between the United States and China reflect this term?
2. How does this co-dependent relationship affect how the United States criticizes China's record on human rights? Do you think this is right?

Ordinary Americans left out of bailout
October 27, 2008

Mark Seifert tours reporters around streets more reminiscent of Baghdad than Cleveland, Ohio.

They are deserted. The homes are boarded up, covered in graffiti. Once residential neighbourhoods, they are now hangouts for drug dealers.

At the end stands a nice, little ranch with a kept garden. It's the home of an elderly couple who have lived here for decades. Their mortgage is paid off but the value of their home has depreciated by half. They cannot sell. They have nowhere to go.

"You really have to feel for them. They are all alone here," says Seifert. "It's a war zone."

War zone, indeed. When the executive director of Empowering and Strengthening Ohio's People holds tours for veteran journalists, they are blown away. One journalist who covered Hurricane Katrina said the streets looked like New Orleans – the only difference after Katrina were the marks labelling which houses had bodies inside.

"Black, white. Young, old. It's affecting everyone," says Seifert. "This is America."

You can hear the frustration in Seifert's voice. The man has every right to be frustrated. For years, Seifert has worked with people facing foreclosure due to subprime loans. Despite his hard work, the crisis has spread beyond Cleveland's borders and into the heart of the American dream.

Seifert's story goes back to 1999 when his organization focused on lobbying efforts like getting more crossing guards. Suddenly, residents stopped coming to meetings. Seifert called to ask why and found their phone lines were cut. The community members were losing their homes.

"We didn't even know what predatory lending was at the time. I don't think it was a term that was used," he says. "But we knew we had a problem."

Quickly, Seifert changed his focus. Rather than lobbying for crossing guards, he was throwing plastic sharks on the lawns of bank executives to protest lending practices. His organization doubled its staff, hiring loan counsellors to renegotiate mortgages and prevent foreclosure.

But, Cleveland was only the epicentre of the growing battlefield. There, entire neighbourhoods were foreclosed while Seifert's organization was overwhelmed by mortgage workouts, going from 1,500 in 2007 to almost 3,700 in 2008.

Seifert watched what he says could have been prevented.

"What we're talking about isn't rocket science," he says. "I mean, wake up guys. You shouldn't have been making loans without asking for a paystub. With that one little thing, we could have stopped the crisis.

"Now, it's destroying our economy and it's being exported around the world."

In the end, Seifert places the majority of the blame on the government. He says they could have taken action by regulating the industry rather than ignoring the problem until it affected a less marginalized population.

"This became a crisis because white, middle-class people started losing their homes," he says. "Before that, nobody gave a damn. When it was predominantly lower-class African-Americans, nobody cared."

What Seifert can take solace in is the fact his organization has an 85 per cent success rate in renegotiating mortgages. Through their mortgage counselling program, they have been able to negotiate monthly interest rates to ensure people can keep their homes.

Small victories, but nonetheless important on this economic minefield.

All the while, Seifert watches while the government draws up a $700 billion bailout to save the biggest casualties. Not enough, says Seifert. The bailout may help the banks but does nothing for ordinary Americans who have been left homeless as they struggle with their mortgage payments.

These are people who wanted a home. People who were simply living the American dream.

"We just don't think people should have been set up to fail," he says.

Discussion Questions:

1. Throughout this crisis, why do you think we heard more from

CEOs of companies and investors rather than people who were losing their homes?

2. What are some of the implications of an entire neighbourhood being deserted?

✱✱✱

Investing for profit – and for good
November 17, 2008

Steve Schueth might abstain from alcohol, tobacco and gambling. But, he's not trying to convince you to do the same.

"I don't consider myself a missionary," he says. "We are not out to convert anyone."

Instead, Schueth's disciples find him. They believe he can line their pockets with the power of good rather than greed. And, as the rollercoaster ride once known as the stock market continues on another course of ups and downs, Schueth isn't doing so badly.

Schueth is no preacher and there's nothing pious about his work. As president of First Affirmative Financial Network, an independent investment advisory firm working in the field of socially-responsible investing, Schueth puts together portfolios that integrate profitability with personal values.

"It's about investors wanting their money to do double-duty," he says. "Investors who want their money to make money and make a difference."

The idea hasn't been an easy sell on Wall Street. But, the financial crisis has changed the playing field. Socially-responsible portfolios have experienced losses like everyone else. But compared to their competitors, these funds haven't sunk quite so fast.

"We've been hit. Everybody's down," says Schueth. "But, based on what I've seen so far, both in terms of our own portfolios and others I'm following, we're down less than most of our conventional competitors."

The numbers speak for themselves. Year to date, the Dow Jones has plummeted 33 per cent. Compare that to Parnassus Workplace, a socially-responsible investment fund specializing in companies

122

with good management and employee relations. They are down 25 per cent. On the opposite end of the spectrum, the ISE SINdex (yes, it's real) which specializes in supposedly recession-proof alcohol, gaming and tobacco stocks, is down 43 per cent.

But, it's not just competitive returns drawing people to socially-responsible investing – it's the desire to do more with your money.

Traditionally, the generous investor might donate part of his yearly return to charity. But, where does that money come from?

In the past, it was SINdex stocks that produced big returns despite the obvious social consequences.

For some, that idea didn't sit well.

"It's like the Catholic going to church on Sunday but being a sinner during the week," says Schueth.

So emerged socially-responsible funds built from the grassroots by investors who wanted more from their money.

The investment formula is a little more advanced. Rather than just looking at profit margins and annual returns, extensive research is conducted into the quality of the company.

"There's now a whole other layer of research," says Schueth. "And, it's something that's helped us avoid exposure to certain areas."

Most notably was Enron. The company's business practices didn't live up to the standards of a socially-responsible company. So, it wasn't included in Schueth's portfolio. More recently, it was companies like Lehman Brothers and AIG – two of the biggest casualties of the credit crunch.

"There are different reasons why these companies didn't appear in socially-responsible portfolios," says Schueth. "But a huge amount of it can be traced back to transparency."

Schueth explains the two companies didn't meet the funds standards for good business practices in their qualitative research. That has saved them from some major losses.

The philosophy is simple. Companies with smart, forward-thinking environmental and social policies developed them with smart, forward-thinking management teams. These companies tend to have better relations with employees, mitigate risk and build customer loyalty based on ethical values.

As an investor, it's easy to be tempted by the supposedly

recession-proof stocks that don't sit well with our conscience. But, at a time when excessive greed has caused the worst financial crises since the Great Depression, it might be time to confess our sins, repent and readjust.

Discussion Questions:
1. Why do you think industries such as alcohol, gaming, tobacco and weapons have produced big returns for investors in the past?
2. Have you ever considered how you might invest your money for the future? What factors are important when determining what companies you want to invest in?

✳✳✳

A better way to track economy's health
January 26, 2009

It's about time we start doing a little more to rev up the economy.

Here are some suggestions. Get a divorce. Drive over the speed limit possibly resulting in a collision on a major freeway. Sink an oil tanker so we can clean up the mess.

Not the most desirable actions for our social welfare, but in the sometimes-weird world of economics, economists will be cheering.

No offense meant to any of the economists we know. But, how on earth is this helping? As the global financial crisis (GDP) leads us down the road to recession, the gross domestic product is our guide. Recession is defined as two consecutive quarters of negative growth in GDP – and car accidents and natural disasters are contributors to that all-important number.

When GDP says it tallies the total market value of all goods and services produced within the country, it means everything. But, when it tries to measure our economic health and well-being, the number falls short.

Introduced in World War II to measure how much of the economy could be put towards wartime production, GDP quickly developed into our primary economic indicator. But, that was never its original purpose.

Simon Kuznets, the economist who helped standardize the measurement, said in 1962, "Distinctions must be kept in mind between quantity and quality of growth."

Unfortunately, we didn't heed his warning – a warning that could have prevented our current mess.

As industry has grown, so have the problems surrounding it. Unbridled consumerism at home and the one-dollar-a-day wages overseas both contribute to a nation's GDP. A forest of trees contributes nothing. Clear-cut that forest and the economy swings into high gear.

"Some of the expenditures don't make anyone better off or even keep our current welfare intact," says John Talberth, director of the sustainability indicators program at Redefining Progress. "But there are also benefits that aren't included in GDP – parenting, housework, volunteers. Those are our quality of life."

Other indicators do take these socially-positive actions into account. Those indicators tell a different story. The Genuine Progress Indicator broadens its scope to account for the societal costs of some monetary transactions and the benefits of some non-monetary transactions.

"In a nutshell, it gives a dollar amount to beneficial activities that wouldn't be recorded in GDP," says Talberth. "It also puts a negative cost on things like environmental degradation, the time we spend commuting and loss of our natural resources."

It also puts a dollar value on accumulated debt and borrowing – factors that have been leading causes in the current financial meltdown.

"GPI realized that the more we borrow, the less sustainable it is," says Talberth. "You can't borrow forever."

When those figures are calculated, the two indicators show very different routes to recession.

GDP per capita has more than doubled in the United States since the 1950s as many Americans live the dream of a television, two cars and a house in the suburbs. When GPI takes into account the environmental costs and the debt families have accumulated to pay for that dream, the indicator has dropped 45 per cent since the 1970s.

Like Kuznets said, there's a distinction between quantity and quality. Had we heeded his warning, we could be in a very different spot on the economic map.

Obviously, no economist is cheering for oil spills. We know some wonderful economists who recognize that a stay-at-home mom is contributing more to the economy than building another prison. So why are we letting these monetary transactions be the primary definition of our progress?

We all know that money isn't everything. By going beyond our gross domestic product, maybe we can start solving our gross domestic problems.

Discussion Questions:
1. Think about some of the volunteer work, fundraising or campaigning you have done in the past. How has this service helped contribute to a better world? Do you think it should be included in assessing the health of the country?
2. What is the significance of quality versus quantity? Why does this matter when looking at the health of the economy?

✳✳✳

Food deals leaving developing nations hungry
December 28, 2009

In 2009, the World Food Programme imported humanitarian aid to about 5.9 million people in Sudan.

The conflict-stricken nation is one of the organization's largest projects. Civil war and ongoing violence have destroyed the country's infrastructure and uprooted its population. That makes sustenance farming virtually impossible and leaves millions facing starvation.

But as food aid stamped with the World Food Programme's logo is shipped to Sudan, thousands of tons of wheat and rice are shipped out.

This food won't end up on the world market. It has specific

destinations: Riyadh, Beijing and Seoul to name a few. That's because 840,000 hectares of Sudanese farmland is currently leased to the governments of Saudi Arabia, China and South Korea. They use it for the sole purpose of feeding their growing populations.

Still, Sudan isn't able to feed itself.

"We have millions of acres of land, very flat and unspoiled and it hasn't really been even explored yet," Sudan's Minister of Finance, Tarek Shalabi, told *Bloomberg* in December. "Sudan is a very good place for agricultural investment."

Land grabbing, as it's called by opponents, is a new phenomenon. Since 2007, the Gulf States as well as wealthy Asian nations have bought land across the developing world to grow food staples to ship home. But, many of the countries from which they are buying are not food secure themselves.

The trend grew out of the food crisis. When commodity prices soared, arid nations in the Middle East and countries with large populations began searching for cheaper imports.

"They lost faith in the international market's ability to take care of food," says Devlin Kuyek, a researcher with GRAIN, a non-profit that supports small-scale farmers. "They took a more aggressive approach by looking for ways to buy up farmland for their own food needs."

Through government-backed corporations and sovereign wealth funds, the World Bank estimates 50 million hectares have been bought for food production. That's roughly equivalent to half of China's farmland. The deals are private so details are difficult to identify. But, most acquisitions are long-term leases, concessions or outright purchases ranging in length from 30 to 99 years.

China and the United Arab Emirates have already secured deals with the Democratic Republic of Congo and Senegal respectively. In September, Ethiopia said three million hectares were for lease.

But, with Congo facing widespread unrest, 20 per cent of the Senegalese population officially hungry and 13.7 million Ethiopians in need of emergency food aid, many fear these backroom deals will exacerbate the problem.

"In those places where we've seen the deals going forward, there has been displacement, loss of access to pastoral lands," says Kuyek. "And the jobs these companies are creating have been extremely low paid. They are under some of the worst conditions in the world."

GRAIN estimates workers at an Ethiopian farm owned by Indian producers make 70 cents per day. Local farmers have lost their grazing and farmland. Their protests have been put down by police.

"There is a lot of manipulation and zero consultation," says Kuyek. "It goes contrary to any notion of food security and what's good for the local population."

During the financial crisis, food inflation dropped from a peak of 18.2 per cent in August 2008 to 4.7 per cent in November. But, economists worldwide warn that as the recession eases, prices will start creeping higher. In preparation, Kuyek says we need to secure food for everyone.

Food and Agriculture Organization Director-General Jacques Diouf noted in a meeting at their headquarters that "private investment should be encouraged." But, he added the deals must reflect the needs of developing countries by ensuring fairness and sustenance for local populations.

"We need a food system that looks after people's needs," says Kuyek. "It's not good for countries to go out and secure their own food needs in countries suffering from hunger."

Discussion Questions:
1. If Sudan is one of the World Food Programme's largest recipients of aid, should the country's finance minister sell its farmland to other nations?
2. A country such as Saudi Arabia has very little farmland of its own. What are some ways for it to ensure food security without jeopardizing supplies in another part of the world?

✳✳✳

Iraq Stock Exchange: High-risk investments
February 21, 2010

Trading floors are known for being volatile. Those who think they're tough should try navigating the Iraq Stock Exchange.

On Jan. 12, the Tuesday trading session was cancelled. Intelligence reports pointed to a planned suicide attack somewhere in the capital. As a precaution, authorities ordered a strict curfew on Baghdad.

"The stock exchange has called off its session on Tuesday because of the inability of its employees to reach their workplace," a source told the *Aswat al-Iraq* news agency in a bit of an understatement.

And New York City investors thought midtown traffic was inconvenient.

This isn't the first time Shwan Taha, CEO of Rabee Securities, one of Baghdad's oldest and largest brokerage firms, has seen trading suspended. Of course, it's nothing compared to 2006 when it lasted for months during what the United Nations called a "civil war-like situation."

Today, Taha sees that relatively more security in the streets means the same for his investments.

"On the exchange, the largest sector is by far the banks," he explains while e-mailing stock reports over a problematic Internet connection. On this day, the Bank of Baghdad closed at 1.98 Iraqi Dinars – less than a penny USD.

"Then there is the tourism sector," he says. "But, that's really more real estate when you get into it."

Taha knows the intricacies of this market. After all, he has traded shares in Baghdad since its first exchange opened in 1992. Back then it was the Baghdad Stock Exchange. Under the rule of Saddam Hussein it provided a prosperous living.

"It operated well until the invasion at which point it was closed. Then squatters moved in for a year," says Taha. "The U.S. tried to reopen it. But, reopening was a fanciful thing. They couldn't manage it. They were incompetent."

Without a formal system of trading, brokerages set about creating their own private exchange. In June 2004, the Iraq Stock Exchange opened with 15 listings. Today it has about 90 companies and moved to electronic trading.

"It's the same system that the NASDAQ uses," says Taha. Although, he acknowledges it can't rely on the country's battered power grid that leaves Baghdad in the dark unexpectedly and for long periods of time. "You have to factor in that the computer system and servers can't go off. So, the exchange runs on generators. Trading only happens for two hours a day."

As a back-up, the old system remains in place – whiteboards and dry-erase markers. Throughout the exchange building, a former restaurant in the heart of Baghdad, hanging boards represent each company listed. Traders, mobile phones pressed to their ears, crowd these boards, writing and erasing notes to buy and sell.

It's a definite skill that requires a fast hand and a shrewd eye. Now though, investors can verify their trades on the spot rather than waiting two weeks for certificates. That's something Taha hopes will bring in new investors.

"We definitely cater towards foreign investment. We've seen an uptick, especially frontier funds," he says. "But, the global custodians of the economy have not been to Iraq yet."

Iraq is still tiny compared to established markets in London and New York. By the end of 2008, the ISX had traded only $270 million compared to the NYSE's $16.7 trillion. But, in spite of the non-market volatility, many hope local and foreign investment will boost the nation's economy.

On the last day of January, despite the delay earlier in the month, the index was up 1.16 per cent. As Taha predicted, the banks dominated the trading. But, Tourist Village of Mosul (HTVM) represented one of the biggest gains, up 10 per cent on the day.

For people like Taha, this only proves there's money to be made at the ISX. Of course, the investment may be a little more high-risk than usual.

Discussion Questions:
1. Think about your personal use of technology. If you were only able to use it for two hours a day, how would you adapt? How would our economy be different?
2. How would investment in business help development in Iraq? What could be done to make investors like Taha more secure?

8
The Environment

At 12-years-old, Severn Suzuki stood up in front of a group of politicians and dignitaries at the 1992 Earth Summit in Rio de Janeiro, Brazil.

"I'm only a child, yet I know we are all part of a family," she said. "Five billion strong, in fact, thirty million species strong and we all share the same air, water and soil – borders and governments will never change that.

"I'm only a child, yet I know we are all in this together and should act as one single world toward one single goal."

In the nearly 20 years since she delivered this famous speech, the only thing that has changed is the fact that our family has grown to a little over 6.5 billion strong. We all still share the same air, water and soil. Yet, these elements continue to be wasted, polluted or spoiled by careless habits.

As Severn said herself, the environment is an issue that knows no borders. It demonstrates just how interconnected our world is. It's essential that the next generation understands this concept.

The problem of global warming goes beyond the temperature rising. It's a product of our lifestyles in the industrialized world and it is currently causing droughts and unpredictable rains in sub-Saharan Africa. Those weather patterns devastate the crops grown by the region's people, increasing levels of poverty.

Because of this poverty, we have witnessed high incidences of child labour, conflict over scarce resources and the worsening of other environmental problems like erosion and deforestation. This in turn exacerbates the global warming problem and the cycle continues.

The theme of interconnectedness is a common thread that runs through each of the articles presented in this section. We think you will find that while each focuses on one person, one town or one country, the issue and its effects penetrate borders and find resonance in your own life.

The other aspect that still rings true in Severn's speech is that young people are at the forefront of this movement. By changing your consumption habits now, speaking out on behalf of the environment and advocating for others to do the same, you can make a difference not just in the world, but *for* the world.

By learning that our actions go beyond borders, we can lead ourselves to a better future.

Toxic e-waste pouring into Third World
April 21, 2008

Have you ever wondered what became of your VHS player? How about that old computer with the black and green monitor, or your first cell phone that was the size of a loaf of bread?

We laugh at the memory of this tragically out-of-date technology, but for the developing world, our old electronic devices have become a very serious problem.

With people constantly upgrading their computers, TVs and cell phones, electronic waste, or e-waste, has quickly become the fastest growing component of solid waste. Compounding the problem, e-waste is often extremely toxic.

Despite international agreements that prohibit the import and export of hazardous waste, shipments of broken electronic devices continue to pour into the harbours of Kenya, India and especially China.

The reason is strictly financial. The U.S. Environmental Protection Agency estimates that it is up to 10 times cheaper to export e-waste than to dispose of it domestically.

Mercury, barium, lead and cadmium are just a few of the dangerous elements that can be found in discarded devices. Many more toxic materials are used in the salvaging process that recovers the gold, silver, copper and other valuable metals found in computers, cell phones and TVs.

Acid baths and open fires are typical of the inefficient and dangerous methods used in the recovery of these precious metals. Toxic fumes and acid spillage contribute to an unsafe working environment. The hazardous elements accumulate in landfills and can leech into the groundwater, leaving it undrinkable.

The Basel Convention – which the United States has yet to sign – is an international treaty that addresses e-waste. While it has helped to slow the transfer of toxic waste between nations, it lacks accountability.

The individual parties of the convention are left to police themselves. So while China, for example, has signed and ratified the convention, there is no international enforcement – and so the practice of importing e-waste continues unabated.

Solving the E-Waste Problem (StEP) in Bonn, Germany, is an initiative of several UN organizations. Despite their efforts to stop the flow of e-waste into developing nations, executive director Ruediger Kuehr, can understand why China continues to accept shipments.

"China, like India and many other countries, is really hungry for resources, so they let e-waste into their country to support their production chain," he says. "They have many people making their living off of e-waste, so they cannot easily say 'Let's stop all of these imports.'"

An estimated 150,000 people are employed by the e-waste industry in Guiyu, China, and in India 25,000 more are working in the scrap yards of New Delhi. The gold, silver, copper, aluminum and other metals they salvage become a vital resource for the manufacturing of new items. The work is as arduous as it is dangerous, and yet a typical wage is only $2 to $4 a day.

Consumer awareness on the issue of e-waste is still low, but on the rise. People have begun to demand "greener" technology, and companies are starting to listen.

In March 2008, Greenpeace released the seventh edition of its Guide to Greener Electronics, providing environmental impact rankings for the industry. Toshiba and Samsung were at the head of the class, improving their recycling programs and using alternative, non-toxic materials. According to the report, Microsoft, Phillips and Nintendo were at the bottom of the group.

While virtually all of the manufacturers had shown some improvement, it's been a slow process by any measure. A significant increase in consumer awareness, elevated pressure on industry to provide solutions and economic alternatives for developing nations are all necessary if we're ever going to dispose of this e-waste problem.

The Basel Convention has still not been ratified by the United States. The protocol currently has 13 signatories, including Denmark, France and the United Kingdom. Canada has yet to ratify as well. The convention will not go into force until 20 countries have ratified the protocol.

Discussion Questions:

1. Why would countries like China and India import e-waste when they know the health and environmental risks?
2. What are some ways you could ensure e-waste is disposed of properly in your home? Are there ways to help solve this problem through your consumption habits?

✷✷✷

Green city to rise in the desert
May 5, 2008

A new kind of oasis is forming in the middle of the desert.

In one of the harshest environments imaginable, where temperatures regularly rise to 50 degrees Celsius and sandstorms can limit visibility to a few metres, construction has begun on what will be the greenest city on Earth.

Abu Dhabi is leading the way in developing the world's first solar-powered, car-free subdivision. Called Masdar City, the initiative is harnessing the region's enormous wealth, along with its zeal for glitzy construction projects, to build an entirely eco-friendly community of 50,000 people right in the heart of the Persian Gulf.

If successful, Masdar City will become a haven for green living in one of the most polluted areas in the world. More importantly, it will serve as a model for what's possible when governments and business leaders work together to combat global warming.

The city's plans are nothing if not ambitious. From futuristic pods that transport residents to work on solar-powered magnetic rails, and state-of-the-art composting and recycling facilities, developers are already billing Masdar City as the world's only zero-carbon, waste-free city.

Produce will be grown in local greenhouses and fresh water will come from a nearby desalinization plant. What's more, buildings will have to adhere to strict energy conservation regulations and air conditioners will be powered by wind towers.

Masdar City is expected to cost more than $20 billion and will take a decade to complete.

While it may seem a little ironic for a place that relies almost exclusively on oil wealth to be building a car-free city, Abu Dhabi's project is an important step toward developing alternative energy technology. With gas prices soaring, supplies dwindling and concerns over global warming now front and centre, our reliance on oil has again come under intense scrutiny. But progress on breaking this dependence has been painstakingly slow.

That's why Masdar City is only one element of Abu Dhabi's push toward clean, renewable energy. In 2006 the United Arab Emirates capital launched its Masdar Initiative (Masdar means "the source" in Arabic), a multi-billion dollar investment into the research and development of environmentally-friendly technology, such as solar and wind power.

In the hope of becoming a leading producer of green energy solutions, Abu Dhabi has even partnered with the Massachusetts Institute of Technology to build a graduate-level university, dedicated to the study of alternative energy, right in Masdar City.

"For an Arab oil country to start this kind of research, it actually makes a lot of sense," says Lester Brown, founder and president of the Washington-based Earth Policy Institute. "Besides oil, the one really abundant resource they have is sunlight."

Abu Dhabi's dedication to alternative energy is to be applauded. Most countries may not have the money for elaborate technology like magnetic pods, but simple environmental measures aimed at greener living are within reach for any government willing to invest in them.

Sweden, for example, has committed to breaking its dependence on fossil fuels by 2020 through a series of eco-incentives, such as tax relief for homes and offices that convert to renewable energy.

This makes Canada's continued dismissal of the Kyoto Protocol even more dismaying. We already know how to combat global warming – Masdar City and Sweden are prime examples – but without similar concrete government commitments, action becomes impossible. Canada is losing out on the economic benefits of being a leader in the development of green technology, something the country is certainly capable of.

Back in the desert of Abu Dhabi, only time will tell if Masdar

City lives up to its idealistic projections. But by seeing how government and business leaders have gotten on board with the city's green initiatives, it's already clear that their intentions are no mirage.

Construction of Masdar City began in 2008 with the first buildings set for completion in late 2010. Despite the economic crisis, the project, which will cost anywhere from $10 to $30 billion, is moving forward. The city is reportedly five to 10 years away from completion.

Discussion Questions:
1. What could be done in Canada to encourage large-scale environmental projects like Masdar City?
2. What would motivate a country like the United Arab Emirates to take on a project of this scale? What makes it feasible?

✳✳✳

U.K. village at forefront in fight to ban plastic bags
September 22, 2008

Welcome to Modbury, England, population 1,500.

It's a quiet town in the Devon hills not far from the sea. There are three churches, three pubs, a market and absolutely no plastic bags.

That's right. This small village carries the distinction of the first town in the British Isles to ban plastic bags.

The story began when local filmmaker Rebecca Hosking witnessed the environmental devastation caused by thousands of bags while filming on Hawaii's Midway Island. There, animals often mistook the bags for food.

Hosking made a documentary for the BBC and showed it to the town's merchants. One night at a pub over a few lagers, she suggested to some retailers the idea of a ban. Word spread and within a month, the merchants met. By show of hands, they voted to ban the bags.

Given, Modbury doesn't have a huge environmental footprint to begin with. But, the town's impact has been huge.

Modbury took its message to anyone who would listen. It made international headlines, won an award from the World Wildlife Fund and hosted delegations from cities looking to implement their own bans.

"We are nothing special," says a statement on the town's website after being inundated with messages. "We just got out there and made it happen in the hope that you would do the same in your communities."

Modbury's ban and a few others, was one of the first blows in the battle of the bags. But outside these centres, the bags still seem to have the upper hand.

Of the estimated 500 billion bags consumed each year worldwide, millions will turn into litter.

Despite environmental concerns, people continue to choose plastic and many governments are reluctant to implement their own bans. Sure, the philosophy of reduce, reuse and recycle will lessen the problem. But, when a simple switch from plastic to canvas could potentially solve it, maybe it's time to go further than the three R's.

Since the 1970s, plastic bags have been a staple around the world. Plastic recycling programs have grown, but the U.S. Environmental Protection Agency estimates that only 5.2 per cent of bags in municipal waste systems are actually recycled.

The result is an increase in the "urban tumbleweed" population as carelessly discarded bags are left to blow through city streets.

Plastic bags do have their advantages. They are convenient, cost-effective and incredibly strong – each one can carry about 1,000 times its own weight in goods.

But, alternatives are far from the holy grail of environmentalism. In Modbury, residents have simply switched to cloth bags for groceries. The town estimates each one saves 1,000 plastic bags. The stores also carry biodegradable, cornstarch-based bags for a charge.

"My personal view is that the disposable plastic bag is the icon of our unsustainable lifestyles," writes Hosking. "I know that removing plastic bags from our lives won't make us a sustainable culture any more than saving the polar bear will stop global warming. However, plastic bags and polar bears will make us all stop and think about the bigger picture."

Modbury isn't alone in banning plastic bags. Developing countries like Rwanda and Kenya have already banned them. So have large cities like San Francisco.

In Ireland, a 33-cent tax on plastic bags implemented in 2002 led to a 94 per cent reduction within weeks. Six years later, cloth is still winning the battle.

The main question that comes to mind is, if all these places are doing it, why can't we?

Far from being just the little town that could, Modbury should be a big influence to all of us.

In the next phase of the battle of the bags, when you're asked paper or plastic, the best answer is canvas.

Discussion Questions:
1. Do you think a similar ban to the one described in this column would work in your community? What steps could you take to make it happen?
2. If alternatives exist, why is it so hard to make the switch?

✱✱✱

Time to take a new look at safe, plentiful hydrogen
December 29, 2008

"The Stone Age did not end for a lack of stone, and the Oil Age will end long before the world runs out of oil."

For the sake of the environment, let's hope that prediction from Sheikh Zaki Yamani, Saudi Arabia's Minister of Oil in the 1970s, was right.

Rising global temperatures and melting ice caps are clear indications of an environmental crisis and the urgent need for an oil alternative. And when you look at the numbers, it's clear that the shift towards a post-petroleum world must begin at the pump.

The United States uses more oil than any other country, over 20 million barrels a day. In fact, they use more than the next four countries on the list (China, Japan, Russia and Germany) combined.

And of those 20 million barrels, 70 per cent is used in transportation.

Hybrids are a step in the right direction, but they're only a stopgap. While they use less gas and have lower CO_2 emissions, they can never get us to our ultimate goal – no gas and zero emissions.

Electric vehicles are a great alternative, especially as we begin to generate more electricity from clean sources like nuclear, solar, hydraulic and wind. But electric vehicles have limited range and will likely never be a viable option for the biggest of the gas guzzlers: transport trucks, cargo ships and airplanes.

But there is a solution. It's safe, green and abundant – hydrogen.

Dr. David Scott, scientist, engineer and author of *Smelling Land: The Hydrogen Defense Against Climate Catastrophe*, puts it bluntly:

"The more you research and the more you think about a post-petroleum world, the more you realize that hydrogen isn't just the best answer, it's the only answer," he says.

Nuclear power and renewables like solar, wind and hydraulic can support our demand for electricity and replace natural gas as the main feedstock in the production of hydrogen.

That hydrogen can then be used to fuel cars, trucks, trains, ships and airplanes with zero CO_2 emissions. It's not a futuristic dream; the technology exists today. Boeing has a hydrogen powered airplane; General Motors, Honda and BMW all have hydrogen cars; and let's not forget: we flew to the moon on hydrogen!

The biggest stumbling block for a conversion from gasoline to hydrogen is the old chicken and egg problem.

There's no market for hydrogen fuel cell vehicles because there's no infrastructure in place to make them a viable option for consumers. Building the necessary web of refuelling stations is possible, but not without billions in investment, and nobody is willing to put up money before there's a market.

That's why mass transit has to take the lead.

"If the G8 countries said that by 2012, every airport had to have hydrogen refuelling stations, we could have all the major airlines switching to hydrogen," says Dr. Scott.

Trains and ships are also great starting points. Since they adhere to specific routes, building refuelling stations becomes a much more manageable job. Gradually the infrastructure can spread, and hybrids can be replaced by hydrogen fuel cell vehicles.

It's a process that could take two decades or more, which is why we don't have any time to waste.

We are in the midst of an environmental crisis, but if we ensure that our oil alternatives are eco-friendly, we can overcome.

We haven't run out of oil just yet, but we can't afford to wait until we do.

Discussion Questions:
1. This column describes a dilemma in which there needs to be infrastructure to build a market, but a market needs to exist to encourage infrastructure. How can we work past this? Who do you think needs to take the lead?
2. If about 70 per cent of our oil usage goes into transportation, where does the other 30 per cent go? What other products or services do you use that require oil?

***

Need to shift focus on Africa's drought
November 2, 2009

Headlines rarely do a story justice – especially when it comes to the words: "Drought in Africa."

They don't capture the feel of the crumbled, arid soil that cannot nourish even a subsistence crop. They don't explain how parched husks of corn can be peeled back to reveal the plant never

141

produced any kernels.

Headlines cannot begin to explain the impact of the drought on the daily lives of individuals living in the region.

But Faith, a mother of four, can.

Even though news is starting to report that drought is becoming more frequent, this only tells of something Faith has been witnessing for years.

Faith's local water source has dried up. Because of that, she was forced to pull her 13-year-old daughter from school to help her make the four-hour, daily hike across the barren landscape to a new one.

This wasn't an easy choice. She had already left an abusive husband in hopes of making a better life for their kids. In seeing her rub her aching knees while resting on a 20-litre jerry can, it's clear the drought is challenging those plans.

That's something a headline really can't explain.

In the 25 years since images of famine in Ethiopia elicited a massive humanitarian response, droughts have become increasingly frequent. They dry subsistence crop. What little rain does fall usually washes away the precious seed. Further, it dries up water-sources for families like Faith's, forcing them to go to extreme lengths to find new ones.

This isn't a one-season phenomenon. Climate experts even predict that by the 50th anniversary of the 1984 famine, drought will be the norm coming three out of every four years.

While headlines focus largely on relief aid, measures to prevent some of the worst effects of drought would be both more efficient and better for Faith's family.

Faith's limited water supply means her two-year-old must be bathed in a nearby dam. The water is used by the region's dehydrated cattle to drink. But, the murky, orange colour is telling of the potentially deadly waterborne illness her son is exposed to.

For her middle children, boys aged seven and four, they are missing out on meals. This lack of nutrition can be devastating during these integral years of growth. Then there is Faith and her elder daughter whose pre-dawn trek puts them in constant danger.

According to Oxfam, just 0.14 per cent of overseas assistance is allocated to disaster risk management, an area of aid that identifies threats together with communities and works to mitigate them. This includes investment in infrastructure that would move food relief around a country rather than importing it and water conservation projects that would help sustain crops.

Unfortunately, the tendency is to give after a crisis rather than take steps to prevent it from happening.

Disaster relief is only a temporary solution and not something that can efficiently be given season after season. With Oxfam estimating it costs approximately $2 (U.S.) to ship $1 (U.S.) worth of food aid, we have to question if there is a better way. Seeing as most subsistence farmers rely on rain rather than irrigation to feed their crops, it's inevitable that the next drought will have the same consequences.

Preventative measures would mean more options for Faith and her family. They would help her prepare for the coming years of drought so that her family does not need this costly kind of aid.

Further, it would empower her to create the better life she dreams of.

But, to do that, we must start recognizing what's already evident to her – that this disaster is now becoming the standard. Only in treating it that way can we work at mitigation.

Discussion Questions:
1. After reading this column, do you think the drought in Faith's community is a disaster or the norm? What is the difference?
2. What is the difference between disaster relief aid and disaster prevention aid? What do you think is needed in this situation? Why?

Growing middle class
spells trouble for climate
November 23, 2009

December's climate talks in Copenhagen have the blogosphere atwitter with commentary – optimistic, cynical and everything in between.

Parthasarthy Guha tells a different story.

Guha doesn't analyze emissions targets or backroom dealings. But, his description of buying his first car is nonetheless telling of the issues facing the meeting.

The post is part of an advertising campaign for the $2,500 Nano by Tata Motors, also known as "The People's Car." In it, Guha describes himself as a car lover – he just admires them from afar. For the last 30 years, Guha's family couldn't afford the luxury. In 2005, he bought a scooter. But, the small, cheap car offers more room for his family.

"Tatas understood our problems and made this car for scooter owners like us," writes Guha. "This made me sure that the middle class people of India can expect something great to come their way."

Guha is the face of India's growing middle class. They are 200 million people strong and are fast becoming an economic powerhouse. They could, however, throw a wrench in Copenhagen's plans.

A middle class is vital to a country's stability and growth. But, as Guha and thousands more upgrade, their effect on the environment, the price of oil and other consumer goods could be enormous.

India's middle class is still different from its North American counterpart. Several definitions abound but the World Bank identifies the global middle class as those earning between $10 and $20 per day. That's a far cry from the U.S. 2008 median household income of $50,303.

Between 1990 and 2002, the World Bank estimates only 80 million people in the developing world entered the Western middle class. But, 1.2 billion joined the global middle class definition. The vast majority of that growth occurred in Asia. While their salaries are still small, rent and food are relatively inexpensive. That increases the prospect of buying discretionary goods.

Seeing families break through poverty is incredible. But, this discretionary income poses a problem. As 1.2 billion people start spending, the potential for overconsumption in our already resource-drained world could be devastating.

Let's look at food. With more income, consumers in China and India have increased their demand for dairy and meat – items once considered luxuries.

"The buying power of our middle class consumers is increasing," said Indian Food Processing Industries Minister Subodh Kant Sahai at a national conference. "Despite the global financial sector, the food processing sector in India grew in double digits by nearly 14 per cent."

This growth has consequences. Already, corn is more widely produced to feed cattle rather than people. This increased demand drives prices up – an effect that will be felt in our supermarkets and by those still in extreme poverty.

The same is true for other commodities. Just this month, a report by the U.S. Energy Information Administration says China and other Asian nations are rebounding oil consumption. Analysts are predicting another rise in price and subsequently the cost of goods.

As for Guha's Nano, "The People's Car" gets 21 kilometres to the litre. His scooter likely got about 80. That means he will produce more emissions. Add that to the vast stocks of coal India and China are using and the targets being set in Copenhagen become much harder to achieve.

Of course, Guha's carbon footprint is still comparatively small. India consumes more energy overall but Canada uses 16.5 times more per capita.

Still, if the emerging middle class starts following Western habits and we don't start curbing our own, we could have trouble finding enough to go around.

Buying your first car is a major accomplishment – even if Guha has to wait another six to eight months for delivery due to Tata's limited production capacity. But, as he celebrates, we all need to reassess our needs and maybe admire a few things from afar.

Discussion Questions:

1. Even though we want to see families break through the cycle of poverty, why does their extra income pose a problem?

2. In this column, the authors point out that we don't want the growing middle class to start reflecting North American spending habits. What is wrong with our level of consumption? In what ways can you curb your own spending habits?

9
Arts & Media

This past March, we had the opportunity to watch as a group of artists came together in a Vancouver studio to dedicate a song to the recovery efforts following Haiti's earthquake.

Singing the words of a young, Somali-Canadian rap artist named K'naan, they recorded the song "Wavin' Flag" as their contribution to the relief efforts.

"When I get older, I will be stronger. They'll call me freedom just like a waving flag," each artist sang in unison with Haiti at the forefront of everyone's mind.

"K'naan's lyrics in "Wavin' Flag" embody the pain, passion and determination of the Haitian people and lend the hope of a brighter future," said producer Bob Ezrin who brought the artists together and recorded the track.

It was incredible to watch as each lyric told a story and put forth a message. We were again amazed at how people across the country responded to this call for assistance. Just weeks after its release, the song received over 100,000 downloads, its YouTube video recorded over 3.5 million views and a Facebook group topped 100,000 fans.

The arts have long played an important role in activism. For centuries, artists, musicians and writers have all created works that embody a story, connect to people and inspire them to take action. Today, advances in technology have allowed us to share those works across platforms. The increasing popularity of social media exponentially increases the potential for reaching others.

That's why we placed both arts and media in the same chapter of this book. Increasingly, they are becoming more interconnected. Through these columns we hope to demonstrate how this changes the cultural landscape, and how it can be seen by some oppressive governments as a threat and by others as a potential to create social good.

Rural Africans go wireless
March 22, 2007

Naabala is a traditional East African Maasai warrior. He has a bright red *shukha* blanket draped over his shoulder and a baton-like weapon called a *conga*, tucked in his belt.

As we walk together, his many necklaces jangle as he tells us about his first lion hunt – at the age of 16 – stopping only to show us which plants cure fever and which ones are poisonous.

Then our mini-culture lesson comes to an abrupt end when something unexpected happens – Naabala's cell phone rings. We look at each other and smile at just how out of place his blue Motorola seems in this very rural African setting.

But that's part of a new reality spreading across the continent. From Angola to Zambia, cell phone towers are now as much a part of the landscape as acacia trees and zebra herds. In fact, Africa is the world's fastest growing cell phone market.

From 1999 to 2004, mobile subscribers in the continent skyrocketed from 7.5 million to more than 76 million. By the end of the decade, that number is expected to double.

Everyone from government officials to rural mamas are going wireless, connecting people at an unprecedented pace. In a continent where remote villages are often cut off from one another, landlines are rare and unreliable and hand-delivered messages can take days, the implications of this technological revolution are huge.

The boom started last decade when many African nations privatized phone service and mobile operators began selling inexpensive phone cards. At the same time, used phones from places like Canada and the United States went on sale for as little as $20.

Millions of people – most of whom didn't even have access to a landline – jumped at the chance of having their own phone. Those who couldn't afford one at least knew someone they could borrow one from.

So now rural farmers can call and check prices at local markets to ensure they get a fair deal for their produce, remote health care workers can contact city hospitals in an emergency and small business owners can increase sales by keeping in touch with their customers.

The continent has quickly become much smaller.

Of course, Africa isn't the only place bridging the digital divide. In 1997, recent Nobel Peace Prize winner Muhammad Yunus co-founded a mobile service in Bangladesh called GrameenPhone. It provides low-cost cell phones to people in rural communities who use them to set up their own telephone companies.

The service quickly spread as local entrepreneurs – mostly women – began selling phone service to other villagers. Now rural women are running their own simple telecom businesses from wooden shacks on the side of dirt roads.

A decade later, 10 million people are able to contact distant relatives, find out about employment opportunities and even conduct their own banking – all for the first time.

Back in Africa, similar programs are springing up to help tackle the continent's many challenges. Just last month, leading mobile companies as well as the U.S. government, announced a $10 million project which will allow health care workers in 10 African countries to enter critical HIV/AIDS information from the field into a central database using a standard cell phone.

And in South Africa's KwaZulu-Natal province, rural women have been given cell phones to report human rights violations, as well as spousal abuse.

Despite this growth, only 60 per cent of the continent is covered by a mobile signal. That number is rising though and as it does so too do the chances for further social and economic development.

In 2004, then-British prime minister Tony Blair's Commission for Africa released a report called *The Impact of Mobile Phones* in Africa, which highlighted the success of cell phones in the continent and outlined the possibilities for the future.

"The poor will benefit from improved services and will be empowered by opportunities to engage with government structures," the report said. "In the long term, it will be the norm for government departments to use portable technologies to deliver public and pro-poor services."

These possibilities have led to other technologies being sold in the developing world at discounted prices. In February, the U.S.-

based One Laptop per Child program began selling kid-friendly computers in poor countries for $150. Organizers hope that the laptops will reach 150 million of the world's poorest children by 2010.

So as we move ahead into the digital age, technology can continue to be a brick in the path to development. Of course, medicine, infrastructure and food are still needed most, but technology can serve as a second tier of development on which to build for the future.

And it changes the face of empowerment. Cell phones are giving people control of their own progress – which they didn't have before – and they are finding innovative ways to help themselves.

Rural Africans are gaining a voice, and are using their cell phones to make it heard.

Discussion Questions:
1. In what ways are cell phones a more appropriate technology for rural parts of Africa than landlines?
2. How can the introduction of cell phones improve life in these areas? Do you see any drawbacks?

✳✳✳

Burma's junta finds no laughs in political satire
December 8, 2008

When it comes to comedian Zargana, no one's laughing.

Any person who has ever performed knows how hard this can be. In comedy, moments of silence feel like an eternity.

But Zargana, whose real name is Muang Thura, has a very tough audience. You see, the silence isn't due to lack of skill – his sharp wit has been critically acclaimed. It's not because his words are boring – his writing has won international awards. And, the moments don't feel like eternity.

They feel like 45 years to be exact.

This is because Zargana's audience is Burma and that country's military Junta is less than impressed with his political satire.

Zargana is no stranger to the inside of a Burmese prison cell. But, this time, the comedian, poet and dissident went too far. He was incarcerated for criticizing the government's response to Cyclone Nargis and leading a private relief effort.

On Nov. 21, he was sentenced to a prison term of 45 years with no chance of parole.

That's three weeks after Republican presidential-nominee John McCain appeared on *Saturday Night Live*. That's also two weeks after Tina Fey retired her spot-on impression of Sarah Palin.

Mark Twain once said, "The human race has one really effective weapon and that is laughter." We here in North America have the power to wield that weapon live from New York, every Saturday night. But around the world, it is met with imprisonment and repression.

"It's not enough to say we are lucky to have these freedoms," says Marian Botsford Fraser, programs associate with PEN Canada, an organization that advocates for freedom of expression. "We have to use this freedom to protect people like Zargana and pressure our own governments to stop these terrible crackdowns."

Political satire has long played an important role in the commentary on our political system. Comedy carries with it an element of truth. It makes us think critically and commands accountability. We've seen that through Jon Stewart's criticism of the War in Iraq. Since 1970, the *Royal Canadian Air Farce* has impersonated our leaders, drawing our attention to their policies and making us think twice when casting our ballots.

But, these comedians have done it while drawing ratings and without the fear of imprisonment.

Zargana's story starts off similarly. In the late 1980s, the former dentist (Zargana means "tweezers") began his career as a comedian, appearing on Burmese television farcically detailing the failures of government. His programming received high ratings and delighted fans.

Then in 1988, Zargana was arrested for taking part in the nationwide uprising demanding democracy. He would spend the next few years in and out of jail as the government stepped up its brutal campaign of repression.

Zargana's "crimes" are eerily similar to our regular programming. In 1990, he was imprisoned for impersonating General Saw Maung, former head of the military government. His videos and poems have been banned in public.

His latest offense – the one that carries the 45 year penalty – involved organizing a group of entertainers to provide disaster relief.

"It's just heartbreaking that a man who was actually in the act of helping people was arrested," says Fraser. "He was doing the work the government was supposed to be doing."

You would be hard-pressed to find a person in North America who would label Tina Fey's job dangerous or expect to see Rick Mercer imprisoned (unless it's part of a sketch, of course).

But, it's our job to make sure we don't stay silent. If laughter is our greatest weapon, then we have the tools for change at our disposal.

The world is waiting for the punch line.

After Cyclone Nargis hit Burma in April 2008, the Burmese government denied entry to foreign disaster response experts as well as nearby British, French and U.S. warships, hoping to unload much-needed supplies on the country's shores. International pressure from the United Nations and the Association of Southeast Asian Nations (including India, China and Japan) later paved the way for international aid agencies to enter the country and help the devastated communities.

Zargana's prison term was later reduced to 35 years. However, he and many activists continue to suffer for aiding in the relief effort and shedding light on the government's response to the cyclone.

Discussion Questions:

1. Despite his extensive criminal record, Zargana has received many international awards for his work. What does the world see in his work that his own government believes is unjust?

2. Political satire is a device Zargana uses to bring to light issues

of injustice in Burma. Are there comedians in North America who do the same? Are they effective?

✳✳✳

Risking freedom for expression
August 24, 2008

Suwicha Thakor is a family man.

The 37-year-old shares a crowded home in Nakhon Phanom in north-eastern Thailand with his wife, three children and dependant father.

An engineer by trade, Thakor sent his oldest child, a boy of 16 named Kanchai, to a bilingual school in Bangkok. The boy wants to study computer engineering at university. Although Kanchai is far from home, the family agrees his schooling is worth it.

Unfortunately, Thakor will be away from his children longer than expected.

Kanchai recently returned to Nakhon Phanom and the local school with his brother and sister. His mother Thitima couldn't keep up with her son's school payments.

Money has been tight for the past few months. It might still be for the next 10 years. That's the length of the sentence Thakor received in April for posting two comments on a website deemed insulting to Thailand's monarchy.

"Most of my friends don't know about this. Some people who got wind of it came to ask if I was related to the man who got arrested," Thakor's 14-year-old daughter Kanyawat told a Thai newspaper. "But there's one person who knew I was my father's daughter, and he deliberately asked me aloud right in front of my school."

As Thakor endured the first few months of his prison sentence, a similar story unfolded in North Korea. There, two American journalists were sentenced to 12 years of hard labour for entering the country without a visa. This, unlike Thakor's story, rightly caught the attention of politicians, the media and the public.

Earlier this month, former president Bill Clinton even travelled to Pyongyang to ensure their pardon and bring the women home.

154

Their release was an important victory for freedom of press worldwide.

But, Thakor's story is a setback.

In Thailand, the crime of *lese-majeste* (or defaming, insulting or threatening the King and the monarchy) carries a harsh penalty. In January, authorities matched the IP address on Thakor's computer to two such comments. He was arrested at a friend's home and denied bail twice. Even though his sentence was cut in half because he pled guilty, the procedure for seeking a royal pardon was suspended.

Thakor's crime is something that millions of us in North America do every day. Our press write articles and readers are encouraged to express their views in comment sections.

There, you can share your views. But, unlike Thakor, you probably won't spend the next 10 years in jail for doing so.

Thakor is not a journalist. He has no American passport or friendship with someone from the mainstream press. That means, besides a petition campaign from Reporters without Borders, his story hasn't garnered the political response of the American journalists.

In Australia, a group of human rights activists campaigned to name a newborn elephant in his honour while the Doha Centre for Media Freedom has been helping his family financially. Still, Thitima has been forced to sell many of Thakor's hard-earned possessions.

While Kanchai is closer to home, dealing with the stress of having his father in jail has had repercussions on the bright student's grades.

"I have not been able to concentrate much because I've been thinking about my father," Kanchai told the media.

Thakor may not be a journalist. But, as the Internet changes how news is disseminated, so too does it change the definition of the practice. Thakor was contributing to the debate media is supposed to elicit. Having true freedom of press and freedom of speech means we need to remember the hundreds of others around the world who have been jailed for expressing their opinions.

Thakor is a family man, not a criminal. He deserves to go back home, too.

Discussion Questions:

1. Think about some of the comments on newspaper comment boards, Facebook or Twitter. Would you change what you were writing if the government monitored these postings or could get you in trouble for writing them?

2. If you are writing your opinion in a newspaper comment board, do you think this is considered a form of journalism? In what other ways is technology allowing ordinary citizens to become more involved in the media?

✱✱✱

Charity calls the tune at El Mocambo
October 12, 2009

In the basement of the El Mocambo Tavern, Abbas Jahangiri leads a team of volunteers in prayer.

A floor up, his staff is busy. Bartenders stock the fridge with fresh beers and clear away cases of empties from the previous night. An indie band unloads gear under the neon palm tree marking the historic entrance of the music hall where the Rolling Stones and Elvis Costello once played.

Down the stairs, past rows of canned goods, volunteers bow their heads among deli meats and chopped tomatoes that will soon become sandwiches for the homeless. Jahangiri asks God to bless the food, the poorest of the poor and those suffering in "Darfur, Darfur, Darfur."

In just a few hours, a typical night will begin at this less-than-typical bar. By making sandwiches, pouring drinks and playing music, everyone who enters the El Mocambo's doors works towards the same cause – charity.

"We have about 100 volunteers who come here at different times, after they finish work. It's such a righteous act," explains Jahangiri. "This place has such a unique culture. It's a landmark for culture. I wanted to use the name and the music to push for charity."

This is no "church basement" volunteer group. Instead, the

Toronto music hall works for the volunteers. At the end of the night, when bands pack up and tabs are counted, all of the venue's profits go straight to work as Jahangiri locks his club and takes the sandwiches to the city's homeless.

The volunteers are part of Jahangiri's service organization, Serving Charity. They, along with the venue's bartenders and bands, are integral to funding the group's activities. That includes sandwiches for the homeless in Canada, as well as projects in Vietnam, India and the Dominican Republic.

"Everything Serving Charity does is picked up by the El Mocambo," says Jahangiri. "In that way, we use the aspects of music and fame and finance and turn it into something for charity."

The shows are like small-scale versions of U2's 360° tour. Both band and barman delicately mix social message with music to create positive social change. Socially-conscious lyrics can usually be heard from the street and the space is often donated to charities for fundraisers. Patrons also get a discounted cover charge for donating canned goods.

It's tough work. For Jahangiri, it's all in the name of Mother Teresa.

"She is my inspiration," he says pointing to a poster of her likeness. "When she passed, I yelled at the TV. Then, I took a vow of service to help the hungry, the unloved, the unwanted."

Jahangiri bought the legendary concert hall with the money from his eclectic background. His education made him head of a professional engineering team and his business sense brought success in real estate. As well, years of dance training made him president of a dance studio.

But with the passing of the Calcutta nun, it dawned on Jahangiri how much was lost. In her honour, he bought the El Mocambo, took a vow of poverty and set about attracting people to charity through music.

Music provided the perfect avenue to help the poor having long been at the centre of social change – from the African-American blues artists who spoke against discrimination to the protest hymns of the Vietnam War.

Today, Bob Geldof has found celebrity through humanitarianism. For Bono, music's most famous activist, his current tour dedicates "Sunday, Bloody Sunday" to the people of Iran and holds tribute to Burma's Aung San Suu Kyi during "Walk On."

This interlacing of music and message is what makes the El Mocambo. If some guitars and lyrics entertain people while they make a difference, that's alright by Jahangiri.

"When the people come here to listen to rock, reggae, heavy metal, they have brought charity," says Jahangiri. "That is such a triumph."

Discussion Questions:
1. What is it about music that motivates people to act? Is there a song or an art form that has inspired you?
2. Some people may argue that musicians should stay out of politics. Others believe the arts reflect emotions and issues that are relevant. What is your opinion?

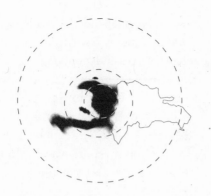

10
The Haiti Earthquake

It was late on a Tuesday night in January when we received a phone call telling us to turn on the television. We knew by the tone of voice that the news wasn't going to be good – but nothing could have prepared us for what we would see.

It was Jan. 12, 2010. A magnitude 7.0 earthquake had struck Haiti, just 15 kilometres from the capital of Port-au-Prince.

We watched the initial images roll in. A small girl – injured and covered in dust – was being pulled from the rubble. It was hard to fully understand the extent of the damage and suffering.

Free The Children had been active in Haiti since the late 1990s. So, our thoughts immediately turned to friends, children, schools. Already Haiti was the poorest country in the Western hemisphere. On a previous visit we remember going to Mother Teresa's orphanage in Port-au-Prince and seeing three babies to a crib because they were so severely malnourished.

Tuesday, Jan. 12 may have been the day of the earthquake. But, Haiti's suffering started a long time ago.

Haiti is a nation founded by former slaves who declared their independence from the French on Jan. 1, 1804.

"Vow before me to live free and independent, and to prefer death to anything that will try to place you back in chains," reads the country's Declaration of Independence, which was unearthed in early 2010 by a student in London. "Swear, finally, to pursue forever the traitors and enemies of your independence."

But, this freedom came at a great price. The French demanded the modern equivalent of $21 billion in reparations, something the country simply couldn't afford. By 1900, 80 per cent of Haiti's budget was going towards debt repayment. The country paid off the original sum plus interest by 1947. But, Haiti was left impoverished and politically volatile. In ensuing years it would amass a new debt of over $1 billion (U.S.).

After a series of occupations and corrupt dictatorships, Haiti's huge debt grew again. In 1995, the World Bank and the International Monetary Fund pressured Haiti to cut tariffs on imported rice. At that time, the country was self-sufficient in grain but the move caused cheap imports from the United States to flood the Haitian market. This cut off a vital source of income for small farmers.

With many unable to compete, they abandoned the fields and moved towards the overcrowded capital's slums, making the population impossible to determine.

With an estimated 80 per cent of Haitian people living on less than $2 per day and unemployment at 70 per cent, many turned to gathering wood to sell as charcoal. The practice led to the deforestation of an incredible 98 per cent of the country. Without natural barriers to protect against floodwaters and hurricanes, Haiti fell into a cycle of disaster, poverty and dependence on international aid.

For the rest of the night, Craig's phone was busy. A group from Free The Children would be travelling to the affected region to connect with local partners, provide assistance where they could and start an assessment of long-term needs. They would also seek and tell the stories of Haitians bravely working through the crisis to protect their families and rebuild their country.

The following is a collection of those stories. Throughout, you'll find a recurring theme of "Haitians helping Haitians."

This has become the motto behind the long-term development effort. In order to break the cycle of dependence that contributed to the devastation of the earthquake, we have to listen to the needs of the people and assist them in rebuilding the country.

Working locally on earthquake relief
January 17, 2010

Our convoy had just crossed the border between Haiti and the Dominican Republic at the town of Dajabón when we picked up a new member of our team.

His name is Kettelen Napoleon, an off-duty police officer who prefers to be called KK.

KK had little hope left when we found him. He had yet to make contact with his family and assumed they were dead. But, the burly man was eager to help. With no central body organizing Haitians, he didn't know how.

Unable to get hold of anyone in the chaos that engulfed Port-au-Prince, KK offered to accompany us as security the instant he heard our convoy was coming.

"*Le pays est brisé*," he told us. "The country is broken."

He had a point. Government buildings and schools were hit by some of the heaviest damage. Education Minister Joël Desrosiers Jean-Pierre reported 90 per cent of schools were destroyed. The city's infrastructure hasn't fared much better. When Port-au-Prince shut down, so did the rest of the country.

Since the Armed Forces of Haiti were disbanded in 1995, there is no military to keep order. Widespread looting has occurred in the streets. At this point, the U.S. Military is trickling in to restore order to the streets and the congested airport. It was being reported 10,000 troops were due to arrive offshore on Monday – three days from when we met KK.

This is the situation we are finding everywhere. For all the promised aid, there is little getting through.

The day prior, our group flew into Puerto Plata, Dominican Republic to a jubilant atmosphere.

There was no cursing over a lack of food or fuel from the tourists who boarded buses destined for all-inclusive resorts. Here, the airport ran smoothly and efficiently while the all-you-can-eat buffets remained stocked and ready for consumption.

We headed out to the stores to buy the supplies necessary for the duration of our stay.

Our purpose in Haiti is to check on the status of the schools

Free The Children built since establishing a presence in the country in the late 1990s. We are also hoping to connect with our partner on the ground, an organization called Partners in Health, to give them medical supplies.

Partners in Health was founded by a doctor named Paul Farmer nearly 20 years ago. Since then, their presence has been invaluable. Partners in Health developed a system of rural health care based on community mobilization. Its hospitals are located in the rural countryside outside of Port-au-Prince and have about 700 nurses on staff.

They were there before this crisis occurred and will be around afterwards. Because they are not a global brand, but doing such incredible work in Haiti, Free The Children has been using its charitable status to raise funds for their work. The next step will be looking at long-term support for education, clean water and alternative income.

We received reports that, since hospitals in the capital were destroyed, Partners in Health was extracting the injured from Port-au-Prince so that they could receive treatment a couple of hours outside the city. We hoped in reaching them that we could provide medical supplies to assist in their work.

Our small convoy made its way to the northern border crossing of Dajabón. We prepared ourselves for long lines and the possibility of having to bribe officials to gain access to the country.

Instead, we found nothing.

The border crossing was a virtual ghost town. No line-ups of trucks brimming with food or bottled water. No doctors waiting to get to an operating table.

The guards, who were all too happy to chat, informed us that there has actually been a decrease in trucks crossing the border. The roads in Haiti are too difficult to traverse so few have arrived intent on leaving. Everyone coming in, they said, was headed to the congested airport at Port-au-Prince.

That's the problem with this strategy of delivering aid. There's no emphasis on buying locally. Not only are North American goods expensive, the logistics of actually flying them to Port-au-Prince, unloading them and then finding security to get them to the people is downright inefficient.

Yet, in the Dominican Republic, aid was available in abundance while the crossing guards sit ready to process shipments.

Soon after we started driving, KK received a call on his cell phone. He answered with trepidation and his face broke as he listened.

His family was alive. His mother, brother, kids. They had been unable to reach him due to clogged cell phone networks around Port-au-Prince. This is a difficulty we could attest to. Already we learned it was easier for us to contact our office in Toronto than it was our partners in Haiti.

It was an emotional moment standing with this burly police officer we had only just met. He made arrangements to meet his family outside of the capital. The city was too unsafe and they planned to head into the countryside.

We agreed to take KK to the meeting point.

KK's was one of the few happy stories we have come across. By this point, search and rescue has ended. Now, we have moved to search and recovery. Mass graves are being prepared to bury the dead. Very few are being found alive in the rubble.

Like KK, those who have survived this catastrophe are eager to help. As our convoy moved along the rough terrain, we came across one man leading his own relief effort.

His name is Guerby Garby Joseph, the owner of a small restaurant. When we met him, he was in the process of organizing three buses into Port-au-Prince.

This was the second convoy he put together. On the way to the capital, the buses were laden with supplies. They came back filled with secondary school children who were in the capital to study. The first three buses weren't enough, so he was preparing to send more.

Along the journey, Guerby came across others who opened their homes to victims of the earthquake. Touched by their generosity, he opened up his restaurant to survivors. Guerby told us he was offering to hire two people who had lost their homes and businesses in an effort to help them build a new life.

For each of these people, disaster relief will be needed long past the immediate crisis. Coming out of this, we need more aid organizations to follow his example.

From KK to Partners in Health to Guerby, they were on the ground before the earthquake struck. Each of them will be here afterwards, working to rebuild the country.

✳✳✳

Haitians emerging as true heroes
January 18, 2010

Mona Pierre was sitting in her Port-au-Prince church when the tremors started.

The congregants looked wearily at each other as the initial panic set in. Her priest took control of the situation with a simple message.

"Stay put and pray."

From the pulpit, Mona says the priest led them through verses until the ground shook so hard they couldn't follow along. Then, they sang.

Amazingly, when the 7.0 magnitude earthquake stopped, the church was still standing. No other buildings around them were upright. But, this one little parish was safe.

To Mona, the congregants were her family in Port-au-Prince. The 22-year-old was studying nursing in the capital having graduated from L'Ecole de Marie Educatrice, one of the first schools Free The Children built in Haiti. Her family – four sisters and four brothers – remained in the region of Hinche on the Central Plateau.

That's where we found Mona as our convoy continued its trek through the battered country. After spending three days on a football field in Port-au-Prince, she had boarded a bus bound for the safety of the rural countryside.

According to Brother Franklin Armand, this kind of decentralization will be key to the relief effort. As the man who drove the bus that got Mona away from the football field, he was doing his part in making that happen.

Brother Franklin is the leader of the Little Brothers and Little Sisters of Pandiassou, a small community in Hinche. As head of the community, he has been encouraging others to open their homes and their hearts to the refugees trickling in from Port-au-Prince in an effort to get people out of the dangerously overpopulated city.

The capital is virtually destroyed. He says rebuilding will be a long-term process and likely the new capital will bear little resemblance to what it once was.

Hinche, with its population of about 500,000, was spared the worst of the earthquake's wrath. We were with him when he received word from the French Ambassador that the community would soon receive between 2,000 and 3,000 tents to accommodate refugees. Now, Brother Franklin says they are prepared to welcome about 500,000 new members to the community.

The hospitality offered by the people in this region is something to behold. Last night, we stayed with the mother-in-law of Erin, a Free The Children staff member who is accompanying our convoy. We slept on the floor of the small dwelling in sleeping bags and awoke to women preparing coffee and fresh bread while the men shared news from the city.

Mona was among the women preparing this modest feast.

She explained that as her congregation made its way to the football field, they came across people searching desperately for family members as well as the wounded and the dead. The priest offered them comfort through prayer. Mona was struck by the desire to do something to help.

She rushed home amidst the chaos to recover a first aid kit she had been given to practice with in her studies. The contents were meagre. But, when she arrived at the football field with no doctors in sight, it was a welcomed blessing.

Donald had his foot crushed in the earthquake. As he attempted to make his way to safety, he caught the injured limb on a piece of jagged metal protruding from a crushed car. Mona found him bleeding profusely.

The petite girl in the beaded, black T-shirt opened her kit and patched the wound. Soon, she was able to stop the bleeding.

Mona's selflessness through this crisis is truly remarkable. It's something we continuously come across in our journey. As the world scrambles to help Haiti, it's Haitians helping Haitians on the ground who are emerging as the true heroes.

Brother Franklin is one of them. He is a mid-sized man with greying hair and a warm smile. Despite being pulled in every direction – by government officials coordinating evacuations and local people looking for support – he still found time to bring us to the Free The Children schools we were looking to check on.

He was happy to report that, except for some minor damage, Dos Palais, a primary school built with the help of Oprah's Angel Network, was still standing and safe for students to use. Remarkably, it had not only withstood the force of the earthquake, but also the numerous hurricanes which have decimated the country in previous seasons.

The small building housed about 450 students from preschool through to Grade 6. As we walked along the rough road for a viewing, we came across a number of the kids in a long column.

Brother Franklin greeted them enthusiastically before making an introduction. These 172 children were orphans who relocated to Hinche over the last few years. Most came from Carrefour, the impoverished town at the epicentre of the quake. Today, they were dressed in their Sunday best – some shoes too big, some dresses too small – for a singular purpose.

As our now massive group trudged along, we came to a small church where they filed inside. Together, peacefully and gracefully, they sang songs of hope for the people of Port-au-Prince. In that moment, not one person from our convoy had a dry eye.

Despite it being a Sunday when we arrived at Dos Palais, about 20 students milled about. We took the chance to ask about their aspirations. Each expressed a desire to help.

Jules and Wilky, both eight, wanted to be priests. They were already practicing by praying for medical assistance for Port-au-Prince.

Annani, 11, wanted to be a doctor and like many kids she expressed a desire to be older. That way she could already be treating the wounded.

Then there was Darlene.

The 12-year-old relocated to Hinche years earlier. She is an orphan because her family didn't have the means to provide for her. When she was little she was left to fend for herself on the streets.

Today, in a pink dress, her hair neatly braided by a friend who sits proudly beside her, she explains she would like to be a seamstress – but not just any seamstress. Darlene has dreams of teaching others the trade. That way, she explains, they will be able to help strengthen Haiti's economy.

We were taken aback by the 12-year-old's big words. But the maturity that shone through her big smile was only just starting to reveal itself.

Darlene explained that she knew her father lived in Carrefour with her siblings while her mother lived in a town called Pétionville. Both towns were incredibly poor. Through reports we have heard, both were levelled.

Darlene turned her head away as she revealed her history. When we asked her if she had a message for her family, she thought for a moment.

"I would ask them if they were well," she said. "I would tell them to lie down if they were hurt."

But, her face clouded over again as she revealed she had little hope they were alive. As tears rolled down her face, her friend, who so neatly braided her hair, moved in for an embrace.

After drying her eyes, the young girl looked up again and explained to us that she was thankful. Had it not been for the orphanage, she might also be trapped in the rubble. She wouldn't have a chance at an education. For that, she is grateful and is preparing to welcome the refugees coming in from Port-au-Prince.

Many, explained Brother Franklin, will live on the school's football field. Soon, it will be transformed into a refugee camp for about 200 families and will be well-equipped to handle their needs. But, just like Darlene doesn't want to be just any seamstress, Brother Franklin won't let this be just any football field.

Instead, it will be a place where people can heal, physically from their wounds, as well as emotionally and spiritually.

It will be a place where they can start a new life.

The indomitable hope
of Haitians amid chaos
January 19, 2010

Marie didn't appear to be injured when we met her at the Partners in Health hospital in Cange.

She was wearing a pink dress with blue and purple flowers. She stared wide-eyed at the ceiling.

The doctors explained that, while she had no physical wounds from the earthquake, she was gravely ill. They were trying to treat her for a heart condition. They believed it was caused by a secondary infection associated with HIV/AIDS.

Here in Haiti, more than two per cent of the adult population lives with the virus and hundreds more are infected every year. Due to the extreme poverty and lack of medical access at the best of times, mother-to-child transmission through breastfeeding or at birth is quite common.

Part of the mandate of Partners in Health is to provide people with life-saving, antiretroviral therapy (ARV). Their system of doing so has been replicated in many rural settings and aims to eliminate barriers to continuous care. If someone on ARVs does not take their medication every day, this gives the antibodies time to build resistance rendering the drugs ineffective.

It's been nearly a week since the earthquake struck. For some, a wait of this length is effectively a death sentence.

Prior to the earthquake, Haiti already had the highest infant, under-five and maternal mortality rates in the Western hemisphere. Partners in Health had been working for years to alleviate tuberculosis and HIV/AIDS. Now, further barriers to clean water, food and medicine are only exacerbating these problems.

This is something we knew all too well. Since coming to Haiti we have been trying to get reports from the street youth centre Erin and her partner Lucas helped found in the coastal town of Jacmel. We were concerned that one of the boys they work with, a young man who goes by his street name Ti Komik, was not receiving his medicine.

Amazingly, after we highlighted the problem through an entry on Twitter, a friend had e-mailed us within hours. She informed us that she knew of a doctor in the Dominican Republic who could help coordinate a truckload delivery of ARVs across the empty Dajabón border.

Daily, we're blown away by the response we are receiving through social networking. But it's not just online – it's through Haiti as well.

The Haitians live by a culture of *zanmi toay*, a culture of helping out friends in need. After years of having little access to electricity, telephones or the Internet, we are amazed by how much information still manages to get through.

When Partners in Health ran out of fuel for their generator, word spread across the island, even into the Dominican Republic. There, a man went door-to-door looking for diesel fuel. He then loaded the valuable commodity into his truck and drove it across the border to help in his own private relief effort.

More remarkable are the 10-year-olds who recognize that the doctors are completely exhausted. They constantly ask, "How can I volunteer?" Whether it is moving supplies or relaying information, their help is critical. The fact that each of them does this work in a calm, precise and mature manner is truly something to behold.

Henry, a young doctor normally based in Rwanda, took us through the hospital to where we could drop off supplies. When we asked what he was doing in Haiti, he said he just wanted to help. Under his guidance, the hospital they set up in a local church was running smoothly and orderly despite open wounds, bones protruding from skin and the exhaustion that marked his face.

Calmly, he introduced us to some of the patients.

Like Marie, it wasn't the wounds from the earthquake that struck each one of us so deeply. It was the pre-existing wounds that really told the story of how much farther this relief effort has to go now that the initial search and rescue is over.

One newborn we found lying in a crib was so malnourished her mother did not want to admit the baby was her child. It wasn't until the other women around her told us that the baby was hers that she ashamedly revealed the truth.

Next to her, another woman cradled her tiny, premature infant in her arms. The baby was born just one day before the earthquake hit. As we watched her clutch the tiny life, we could not help but think of the thousands of other pregnant women due to give birth.

We've heard reports that all of the hospitals in Port-au-Prince were destroyed. Without them, most women will be forced to have their children in the street. Likely, they will lack the proper care and the sterile medical equipment needed to prevent infections like tetanus.

Finally, we came to a woman who had been extracted from a car in Port-au-Prince. Her leg had been completely crushed. Doctors on the scene did a quick job of amputating it at the knee in order to save her life.

Given the circumstances, said Henry, they didn't do too bad a job. Still, there was a lot of work left to be done. She would require an orthopaedic surgeon to properly finish the procedure and the field hospital didn't have one.

Even if they did, they were running short on blood.

Transfusions themselves aren't easy. As we've seen in Africa, it's an incredible challenge to obtain a safe blood supply in a region where HIV is prevalent and reliable testing equipment is expensive and hard to come by.

This woman in particular will recover. The problem is where she will go next.

Many patients who had their wounds stitched or limbs placed in casts are ready to be discharged. Under normal situations, they would return home to recover. But today, they are effectively homeless. What they need now is housing and relocation services that will allow them to start a new life.

For the moment though, the exhausted doctors are letting them stay here. It's not much but many say they are happy just to be receiving treatment. It's that kind of hope that seems to keep order through the chaos in this small, makeshift hospital.

✳✳✳

Community counters desperation
January 20, 2010

This morning, a phone call came in at around 4 a.m.

It was a call that was hours overdue. Through a day of visiting hospitals, orphanages and communities affected by the earthquake, it was always at the back of our minds.

We breathed a sigh of relief at the sound of KK's voice. Two days ago, we left the policeman, who had offered to accompany us as security, in the town of Cap-Haïtien on the northern coast.

Although, he had plans to meet with his family, he decided to turn back to the Dajabón border.

KK is a policeman whose real name is Kettelen Napoleon. When we met him at the border crossing, he offered to accompany our convoy as security. He believed his family had been killed in the earthquake and was looking to help out in any way he could.

It was as we loaded up the aid we hoped to deliver to orphanages and hospitals that he received his family's call. For all of us, it was an emotional moment when the big man's face broke as he learned that his three-month-old was healthy and unharmed.

This morning, we felt that same relief.

Although KK had made arrangements to meet his family outside Port-au-Prince, he was struck by the desire to help out as much as he could in the relief effort. So, the policeman headed back to the Dominican border with plans of renting a truck, filling it with supplies and then meeting us at Mirebalais, a town outside Port-au-Prince.

"I need help," he told us over the phone. We held our breath as he explained he was 30 minutes from our rest stop. But, his truck, laden with supplies, had lost control and careened into a ditch. Now, he needed help getting it out.

We quickly got ready in the darkness. KK's supplies would be significant to the drop-off at the orphanage we planned on visiting that day.

We made our way to the spot he indicated. When we got there, we witnessed a beautiful sight against the morning sunrise. KK and a group of about 30 to 40 people were moving the supplies and lifting the truck out of the ditch.

This is the culture of *zanmi toay*, a truly remarkable sense of community based on the principle of helping your network of friends no matter the situation.

This morning, it came together in full force. Of course, as we sat down for breakfast with KK, we learned this culture was being put to the test given the dire circumstances.

Upon returning to the border, KK found a much different scene than what we had witnessed days earlier.

The crossing guards were now inundated by people trying to make their way into Haiti. Most were individuals whose vehicles were filled beyond capacity. KK joined the line-up with bags of rice, beans and tomato paste – all staples of the Haitian diet. As well, he carried thousands of individual satchels of clean water.

KK patiently waited at the border. After hours, he managed to cross. It was then he realized he would need help with the thousands of pounds of aid he had overflowing from the truck.

The policeman came across a group of men listening to updates on a radio beside the road. Despite the fact that the region was virtually untouched by the earthquake, the power was off and schools were closed. Officials based in Port-au-Prince did not have the capacity to check on the rest of the country and assumed everything was unsafe. This radio seemed to be the only electronic device working for miles.

KK explained the aid was destined for a group of about 1,000 orphans at Petite Place Cazzeau, an organization Free The Children has helped support over the years. A few agreed to come along.

Their help was almost immediately welcome. Within two kilometres, they popped two tires. Jacking up a truck with a nearly one-ton burden was not something the big man could accomplish alone.

KK knew the journey would come with some level of risk. But, he quietly told us the violence was unlike anything the sometimes unstable country had ever seen. Following the 2004 coup d'état, instability was political in nature so more men were armed. Today, people are fighting for survival. Their actions are driven by absolute necessity.

As KK made his way down the road, he came to a bridge where a number of men were waving as if in distress. As he slowed down the truck, they raised sticks and began chanting that the food was theirs.

Quietly, the policeman reached for his gun and unloaded two

warning shots into the air. The action was enough to scare the attempted looters without harming anyone. As KK explained, he understood where they were coming from.

KK hit the gas and made a break across the bridge. He knew he was losing supplies from the bed of the truck. But, the action was enough to get himself, his crew and the remaining aid out of harm's way.

The truck miraculously continued the rest of its journey unscathed. Then, when KK was about half an hour away from our designated meeting point, he heard two loud pops and suddenly lost control of the vehicle.

It was around midnight and the road was pitch black. The truck had blown two tires on the same side and was completely out of control. KK steered the vehicle towards the ditch and soon he and his crew found themselves dangling on the median's precipice.

Fearful that he wouldn't be able to complete his journey, KK and his team set out looking for locals to help unload the supplies and get the truck running again. The community responded in full force. By the time KK called us, the aid was salvaged and ready to be loaded onto our convoy to be taken the rest of the way to the orphanage.

Zanmi toay at its finest.

As we listened to KK's remarkable story, we had to ask why he did it. Why put himself at risk when he could have just met his family outside Port-au-Prince?

He answered simply: "I feel a sense of responsibility to the people of Haiti."

✹✹✹

'200 people. No food. No water. Help.'
January 20, 2010

We met Marie and her husband Ronald on the steps of the Mission of Immaculate Conception convent. The nuns here have long been friends of our organization, helping to give children in the area just outside Port-au-Prince an education.

Today, despite the structural damage, they are providing refuge for families rendered homeless by the earthquake.

Ronald is a tall, thin man and Marie is a voluptuous woman still glowing from her recent pregnancy. Their daughter, three-month-old Manoueshka, sleeps peacefully on a mattress beside us. Without disposable diapers and with no means to clean cloth, the couple set up layers of old sheets on a mattress they were able to pull from inside the convent.

Normally, finding diapers wouldn't be a problem for Marie and Ronald. The couple had good jobs and was quite well-off prior to the earthquake. But their money is tied up in banks which collapsed. They also lost most of their documents when their home did as well.

The bit of cash they normally kept in the house was drying up. They weren't quite sure what they would do next.

Learning this, we couldn't help but sympathize. Most of us in North America keep our earnings in the bank. If we woke up one morning to no power across the country and our institutions gone, our reserves likely wouldn't go far either.

Our convoy is now making its way into Port-au-Prince and the destruction is becoming much more significant. Along the road, what can only be described as camps for internally displaced persons are everywhere. With little room in which to live, the people are crammed together creating walls out of sticks and clothing.

Still, there seems to be solidarity in sleeping outside. Communities are emerging. Children play hopscotch in the dirt.

What we fear now is what happens when the rain comes. This is not the rainy season in Haiti, so sleeping outside is feasible. But, once the rain starts people will likely head inside the unsafe structures. The weight of the water will likely cause more damage.

As we passed one camp, a sign stood out on the road.

It stated simply, "200 people. No food. No Water. Help."

The sign itself was a simple plea for the basic necessities in life but symbolized so much more. There is order and governance emerging in these camps. We've seen no leadership from the government. While the institution may still exist, it has no control.

Going forward though, there will be a voice in these tents. There will be leaders who emerge. Some will be good while others will undoubtedly become gang-like. Still, there will be a voice.

As we headed to the airport, the fuel shortage took on a new dimension. The cars are off the road and there is not a vehicle in sight. But the line-ups at the gas stations are long. They are made up of people crammed together who wait for hours, bodies pressed up against one another, with water jugs that they use to collect fuel.

We came across an aid worker named Jim. He is an American who has lived in Haiti for 15 years. He has a wife and kids in the town of Pignon and is doing his best to help out. Because he has spent time in both Iraq and Afghanistan, we were taken aback by what he had to say.

"Haiti is a failed state."

Jim had harsh words for how the aid was being distributed and expressed how disturbed he was by the lawlessness on the street. He also estimated that only a fraction of the bodies have been found and could only speculate what that might mean for public health in the coming weeks.

That was his main outlook. Not today or tomorrow. What about next week? The month after that? Sure, the camps were organizing in solidarity now. But, how long would that solidarity last as food and water becomes more and more scarce.

To him, this is effectively a warzone without the armies. United Nations Peacekeepers keep order in some areas as if there is a battle going on. This fact worried Erin a little. While their presence is important, she remembered seeing posters in UN headquarters following the 2004 coup stating, "Child prostitution is illegal even in this country."

It definitely raised questions. What kinds of protections would be in place for women and girls as the basic necessities in life remain scarce and desperation sets in?

None of these questions have easy answers. Neither do those of Ronald and Marie.

Back at the convent, the symbols they once turned to in prayer did little to ease their worries. Haiti is a deeply religious nation with 80 per cent of the population professing to be Roman Catholic. Here though, the statue of Jesus had lost an arm, the Virgin Mary cracked in half.

Outside on the hard ground, little Manoueshka still slept silently.

The baby is an American citizen. Marie flew to Miami six months ago to have her and she carries an American passport.

The couple went to the American Embassy hoping to be evacuated. Officials informed them that only Manoueshka and Marie would be able to leave. Ronald would have to stay behind.

We inquired as to what they would do. We received only silence.

Marie looked at Ronald. Ronald looked down at his sleeping daughter.

The question was one she couldn't ask. It was one he couldn't bring himself to answer.

✱✱✱

Eight days later, the aftershocks
January 20, 2010

When we awoke to tremors this morning, the initial response was panic.

Our team had spent the night at an orphanage in Carrefour, the original epicentre of last week's earthquake. Over the last few days, we have been travelling here to deliver food, water and medical supplies.

We have long supported the agency that runs this orphanage. Prior to the earthquake, it was home to mostly boys transitioning off the streets or from jail. Now, it is welcoming children whose parents were lost or injured.

There is a large wall still standing around the compound. The community has started taking shelter in its relative safety.

It's impossible to get a proper headcount on how many people are here. The three people who run the compound are exhausted. Jeff, the man in charge, said they are working diligently at rationing.

He was extremely thankful when the convoy started to unload fuel for the generators as well as food and water. The kids formed a line to carry the packages to the storage area, sometimes requiring two or three of them to a package.

176

In the evening, we unrolled our sleeping bags next to the kids on the ground. As a precaution, everyone was staying as much in the open as possible.

As the sun began to rise at around 6 a.m., the ground started to shake.

Immediately, the children jumped up and started to run towards a soccer field. The force of this aftershock was clearly bringing back memories of the week prior. As the structurally-unsound walls teetered around them, little ones clutched to kids a few years their senior for protection as they ran.

As the ground rumbled on, two young boys stopped and looked back.

On a mattress that had been pulled from inside lay a boy with his leg in a cast. He was unable to get up on the unstable ground let alone run for safety.

His two friends turned back and ran towards him. Each grabbed a corner of the mattress and half running, half dragging brought the injured boy to safety in the open field.

When the grounds stabilized, we were relieved to find everyone safe. But, this further uncertainty only added to the children's worry. They were scared for their safety as well as their future in Haiti. As the morning light brightened the sky, we did our best to reassure them that they were safe. We toured the buildings to see what was still standing.

But, the aftershock confirmed for us something we already believed to be true. While we reassured the kids that physical damage could be repaired and that the rebuilding would start soon, the emotional scars caused by the horrific and often gruesome images they have seen will take much longer to heal.

The kids are all accounted for. But, we had to wonder about the other parts of Port-au-Prince. Many were sleeping on steps in front of their homes in order to protect their meagre belongings. With many starting to sift through the rubble, they had further shifted walls.

While we haven't received confirmation, we know with this tremor that more lives will be lost.

The aftershock brought each child back to the events of the week before. It left them, and us, worried about what would happen next.

Kindness, resourcefulness in the camps
January 21, 2010

Velena's bright-coloured dress stood out against the rubble surrounding her.

The shattered concrete is the remains of a landmark Caterpillar tractor shop that visitors once saw when they got off planes at Port-au-Prince airport. On this day, it bore no resemblance to its former self surrounded by one of the largest camps for internally displaced persons (IDPs) in the area.

Velena, about 7 or 8, led us with determination to her tent. We found it constructed of sticks she and the other children had scavenged with a tarp draped in between.

She is smart and resourceful. Already, she has dug a latrine behind the makeshift home. The kids told us that the Haitian Ministry of Sanitation was coming around regularly to clean it out.

We were relieved to see Velena had taken these measures. In other parts of the camp the human waste was overwhelming. An aid worker told us he was thanking God this is not the rainy season. Haiti already has the highest rates of infant and under-five mortality in the Western hemisphere. The wet weather would only contaminate what's left of the clean water systems leading to a spread in deadly, waterborne illness.

Velena and her neighbours came to the camp from the impoverished neighbourhood of Solino in Port-au-Prince. The few possessions they were able to recover they brought to the camp in tattered pillowcases and old rice sacks.

When we got to her plot, Velena's father Richard was returning with two aid boxes he had managed to retrieve for the family. They were marked with well-known logos like CIDA, USAID and Oxfam. The family crowded around as they opened them.

One box contained personal hygiene items like soap, toothpaste and maxi pads. The other was filled with pots and a few dishes. Velena looked up and asked, "What are we supposed to put inside the pot?"

We visited six IDP camps on this day. Only one had received a food shipment. That's not to say other measures weren't being taken. One man told us that people had been coming around to take names and information. He wondered if that meant aid would be coming.

Getting from place to place in Port-au-Prince is a challenge. Traffic is wild even with United Nations Peacekeepers and policemen directing people. A few inches of space is enough for people to cut you off.

Passing us was an ambulance being escorted by an officer with a loudspeaker.

"You! The yellow bus!" he yelled. "Stop there. Pick-up, go up ahead."

The ambulance appeared to be taking the wounded to the Médecins Sans Frontières (MSF) field hospital. The view inside was blocked with tarps on two sides. Stretchers were set-up at the reception area in front. The doctors administered care as best they could.

This was an encouraging sight. Others were not.

Corpses continue to be pulled from the rubble. Sadly, many remain alongside the road. Those on the street seem to have become immune to these images. People continue by on their mass exodus of the city carrying what few possessions they were able to recover.

Money is running short. Despite that, merchants are out on the street, trying to sell their supplies before they spoil. In some cases, they too are doing their best to find relief. One woman sold day-old hot dogs and small candies for half their usual price.

"People need something to make their children happy," she says before admitting she can't afford to do this much more.

An orange merchant, about 45-years-old, told us she sold oranges on that corner every day since she was a young woman. She carried them in a bright yellow plastic bowl. We watch as she peels the fruit, cuts it into slices and hands it over to her customers with a grin.

She took no money in return.

"I can't let them go hungry or thirsty," she says. "Today I am just happy if I have helped to quench the thirst of a few."

Signs of hope on final day
in Port-au-Prince
January 22, 2010

In the hours leading up to our departure from Port-au-Prince, no one from our group ate from our personal supplies.

Soon, we would be heading back across the Dominican border, back to the airport where tourists board buses taking them to all-inclusive resorts. Knowing that we were heading back to abundance, there was nothing to do but give what we had left to the kids who humbly asked for a single drop of water to quench their thirst.

As we slowly made our way through traffic, we saw the signs posted by people in IDP camps asking for help. Children came up to the windows of our trucks looking for any means of relief.

Through our limited correspondence with family and friends, we have constantly been asked about violence and looting. "Are you safe?" "Is it dangerous?" While we understand the picture painted on television screens is one of lawlessness, we have to stress that these are isolated incidents.

They are acts of desperation.

Instead, kids like the ones who appeared at our windows and stood wide-eyed are more telling. No one is asking for much. They just patiently wait for relief.

We have to wonder how much that patience can be tested. The extent of the damage in Haiti is devastating. Seeing it compound with the already brutal living conditions is beyond comprehension. As we mentioned in previous blog posts, before the earthquake struck, 80 per cent of Haitians lived in extreme poverty. The country has the highest rates of infant, under-five and maternal mortality in the Western world.

But, statistics don't do justice to this tragedy. As we prepared to leave for home, we all asked, "How much more can people endure?"

That's not to say the people we met over this past week are not strong and fiercely determined. Every day, we met community members emerging as leaders. While our help is desperately needed, it's going to be under the guidance of Haitians that this country finds strength.

It is the people organizing the IDP camps and creating signs detailing their struggles who will give voice to the displaced. It's people like Mona, who stitched up a stranger's foot with her nursing school supplies, who will answer their call despite their own pain and loss.

Those such as Brother Franklin will be instrumental in helping others build new homes. He will comfort them as they start new lives. Finally, we hope the boys who turned back to help their injured friend during the aftershock will use that courage to speak up for their country, ensuring they do not get left behind.

Thinking back to the day we crossed the empty Dajabón border from the Dominican Republic, I remember being taken aback by our security guard KK's commitment to volunteering despite thinking his own family was dead.

The moment when KK learned his child was alive is something I will never forget. His words when he turned back alone to gather more supplies for the group of orphans will remain with me forever.

"I feel a sense of responsibility to the people of Haiti," he said.

There is no doubt that each of these individuals will endure. My hope now is that the rest of the world will feel that same sense of responsibility going forward.

The world's response to the crisis so far has been remarkable. But, we need to remember that rebuilding has to be a partnership between North America and Haiti. Unlike the tsunami, Haiti doesn't have profitable resorts that companies will rebuild. It doesn't have a large population of expatriates around the world, ready to send money home.

Instead, given our extensive ties, it's North America that will be instrumental in helping Haitians rebuild their country in the coming weeks, months and years.

We are getting close to the opening ceremonies of the Olympic Games. As the attention of both the media and the public gets diverted, it is absolutely essential that we remember dressings still need to be changed on wounds. Children still need a school in which they can receive an education. People still need safe homes in which they can live and the means to lift themselves out of poverty.

Haiti is already fighting to do just that. On our way through

Port-au-Prince, we passed by the Presidential Palace, its roof completely caved in. Across the road was a makeshift shantytown.

We arrived to find a group of university students gathered at the main gate with a long tree branch and a length of twine. They scrambled to the top of the fence, secured the branch and tied the twine between the posts and the tip.

Together, they hoisted the Haitian flag.

As it was being lifted, the gathering mass spontaneously broke into song. Hundreds of Haitians raised their voices, jumped up and down and pumped their fists in the air. Through embraces, tears and a mix of fear and pride, their love for Haiti was evident.

Today, we are all Haitian. Going forward, we have to remember we are all human. Never can we forget our responsibility to our fellow man.

***

The work is only beginning in Haiti
January 25, 2010

We spoke with a grandmother in Port-au-Prince about one week after the 7.0 magnitude earthquake hit Haiti.

She had white hair and wore a handmade top with a pleated skirt. Despite the exhaustion that showed through the lines on her face, she kept a watchful eye over a number of small children.

"I already told them not to go back inside, never ever to go back," she said. "I also told them that if an aid truck ever comes here that everyone needs to react calmly. Across the street they jumped on the truck and now the aid won't come here."

The kids who received this advice were mostly orphans. Some had been disconnected from parents who were at work when the tremors started and couldn't find them amidst the mass exodus. Others had lost their families entirely.

The grandmother told us that neighbours were taking care of them. They feed them as best they can with what little is available, give them a place to sleep and make sure they are safe. It's an informal foster network that has been set up through each camp we visited for internally displaced persons.

Children are most vulnerable in this crisis. Prior to the disaster, Haiti already had the highest rates of infant, under-five and maternal mortality in the Western hemisphere. On a previous visit to the country, we saw three babies to a crib in an orphanage because they were so malnourished.

Knowing this we have to wonder what will happen to them. Once the immediate, short-term crisis has passed, will they find a permanent home to live? Will they receive an education? What kind of country will be awaiting them in adulthood?

The immediate response to Haiti by the international community has been remarkable. But, as we witnessed in hospitals, orphanages and makeshift camps across the country, this crisis is going to extend well beyond urgent need.

Already, there are only enough dressings to treat wounds one time. There simply aren't enough to attend to cleanings. As well, antibiotics that help stave off infection are in short supply.

No one embodied this need more than a boy named Ti Komik. He had long been a member of a street youth centre in the coastal town of Jacmel run by our friends and colleagues. Ti Komik was born HIV-positive and needed antiretroviral therapy to treat the disease.

For ARVs to be effective, a patient needs to take the drug every day. Missing a dose can cause the virus to build up immunity. That can mean a death sentence.

In the immediate days following the earthquake, we became concerned Ti Komik wasn't receiving this life-saving medication. Through an appeal, we were able to secure the drugs. But, in the coming months he will need the proper nutrition to keep him healthy. In the coming years, he will need hospitals rebuilt to ensure he is receiving care.

Then, when we have finished treating the immediate medical needs of the injured, access to treatment must be built so children do not die of preventable illnesses.

Rather than only cleaning up the rubble of a collapsed school, we need to ensure that kids return and receive an education.

What we are witnessing today in Haiti is truly a tragedy. Worse would it be if we allowed it to continue.

Discussion Questions:

1. Think back to when you first heard about the earthquake in Haiti. What were your initial reactions? In what ways did you want to help out?

2. It is mentioned repeatedly that Haiti was the poorest country in the Western hemisphere prior to the earthquake. How did this level of poverty contribute to the damage caused by the earthquake? How does it make the relief effort more difficult?

3. What is the difference between a hand out and a hand up? What must the Haiti government and its international partners do to create a long-term, sustainable solution for Haiti?

4. In the second column, Darlene says that she is ready to welcome displaced persons from Port-au-Prince into the countryside. This is part of a strategy called decentralization. Why do you think people were being encouraged to move to the countryside? How do you think this might help in the relief effort?

5. Throughout this section, there is a recurring theme of "Haitians helping Haitians." Why is it important that Haitians themselves are at the forefront of rebuilding their country?

6. What is the situation in Haiti today? How often do you hear about the country and the earthquake in the news?

11
Inspirational Figures

When we started Global Voices, we wanted to write about people who inspired us in the hopes that their stories would go on to inspire others.

The following chapter is about just that.

Over the years, we've been humbled to speak with those we have spent years looking up to. It's by sharing their words that we hope to introduce you to their stories, wisdom and teachings.

Mia Farrow often speaks of meeting with families and individuals affected by war in the Darfur region of Sudan. Elie Wiesel, a Holocaust survivor, Nobel Peace Prize winner and author whose books we read when we were young, constantly asks everyone to "think higher and feel deeper." Then, His Holiness the Dalai Lama, a man whose teachings have helped to shape the work we do, speaks of compassion towards our fellow man.

Each of these individual's stories appear in this section as well as a few others who may be less well-known.

There is Frank Meeink. The hockey enthusiast may not be a household name. But Edward Norton, the actor who played him in a movie based on his life, did receive an Oscar nod. That movie, *American History X*, the story of a former neo-Nazi who learns tolerance after serving a jail sentence, is an incredible story. So is

Meeink's description of what happened after the credits rolled.

Then, there is Ray Anderson. His Southern drawl, business suits and kind demeanor gives the impression that he is a successful businessman. He is. But, listen to his ideas on environmental sustainability and how he works them into his company and you'll be surprised to find his success is the result of an unwavering commitment to the environment he cares so much about.

Finally, there is Nicolas Kristof. We have spent years reading his columns that appear in the *New York Times*. His commitment to reporting from ongoing conflicts, ones that most media outlets tend to forget, is truly an inspiration to what news should be about.

As we explained, Global Voices has been a chance for us to share the stories of those people we have had the privilege to meet. We hope that by sharing them, you too can find inspiration, role models, even your passion.

Mia Farrow stars in role as activist
February 25, 2008

She may be a star on the big screen, but only when you meet Mia Farrow in person does she truly appear larger than life.

While it's usually difficult to stand out in a crowd of accomplished aid workers and diplomats, at a recent conference on the Millennium Development Goals in Montréal, Farrow did just that. The actress wasn't being admired for her movie roles, but for her unwavering desire to be a voice for the voiceless.

In recent years, Farrow's name has become as synonymous with Africa as it has with Hollywood. Far from being a casual activist, she is a UNICEF Goodwill Ambassador who has travelled to places like Angola and Darfur to highlight the plight of women and children there, pleading for world leaders to take more decisive action against poverty and injustice.

What we learned about Farrow at this conference is that she promotes her message just as adamantly to her own famously large family as she does to presidents and prime ministers.

"The two R's I've brought my children up with are respect and responsibility," she explained to us in Montréal. "The view I hope I have transmitted to my children is that we are part of a larger family. When one of us is suffering, all of us are suffering."

It's this philosophy that drives her humanitarian work, she says, and is now the philosophy she tries to pass on to her children.

Farrow is no stranger to being a parent. She has 14 children, many of whom have been adopted from developing countries. With every new addition to her household, Farrow recommits herself to being a socially-conscious role model for them.

"Over and over again we try to remind each other of what really matters, that the only time you really own anything is in the moment that you give it away," she said in a soft-spoken, gentle voice. "I think you get a big rush when you give."

Her passion for young people became evident just by watching her at the conference. Farrow gravitated toward the younger attendees, taking the time to speak to each one. She genuinely listened to what they had to say and was more than willing to discuss with them the one topic that still breaks her heart – the ongoing genocide in Darfur.

Farrow has visited the region twice, most recently in 2006, and continues to shine a much-needed international spotlight on a place where as many as 400,000 people have died since 2003.

Since her trips, Farrow has led the charge in calling for a boycott of the Summer Olympic Games in Beijing over China's continued support of the Sudanese government. In February, director Steven Spielberg heeded her calls by resigning as artistic advisor for the Games, saying he instead wants to help the people of Darfur.

Farrow's children have begun following this lead. Her 20-year-old son Ronan is a UNICEF Spokesperson for Youth and has written about his own trips to Darfur in the editorial pages of *The Wall Street Journal* and *The International Herald Tribune*.

Not surprisingly, social justice runs in her family.

Now in her 60s, Farrow shows no sign of slowing down. Citing Desmond Tutu and retired Canadian Lt. Gen. Romeo Dallaire as her real-life heroes, Farrow says she is as committed as ever to her humanitarian pursuits – a role she considers more important than any she's played in a movie – and to instilling in her children what she calls "the joy of giving."

"My career brought me success, fame and fortune when I was still in my teens. And I found those things did not bring me happiness," Farrow said. "Which means I had to begin a search for meaning and happiness."

Clearly she has found them.

Mia Farrow still continues her humanitarian work. Since 2006, she has returned to Darfur several times and writes regularly about the 2011 referendum on South Sudanese independence. She has also since visited Chad to raise awareness about increasing levels of polio in the country and to stress the importance of vaccination.

Discussion Questions:

1. Can celebrities bring about change differently than politicians or activists? How? What do you think about this power of influence?

2. To what extent does philanthropy enter your mind when you think about your future career? What are some ways that you use your skills to make a difference?

Giving hate a bodycheck
June 15, 2009

The last thing we expected from Frank Meeink was a new appreciation for hockey.

Movie buffs may know him as Derek Vinyard, Edward Norton's neo-Nazi character in *American History X*. The 1998 film was loosely based on Meeink's life.

Loosely, Meeink told us at the Reconciliation Forum in Washington, D.C. The real-life version has no cathartic moment or dramatic ending. The true story begins after the credits.

Oddly enough, it involves hockey.

Meeink grew up in Philadelphia watching the Flyers. The games were his escape. At home, Meeink was abused by his stepfather. At school, he was beaten up for being the only white kid.

"Imagine you shook a pop bottle for 13 years," he said. "But I could always watch the Flyers."

But hockey wasn't enough and the 13-year-old found another escape – a hate group.

Using the Bible, the leaders taught Meeink the impossibilities of an inter-racial society. Meeink explains he didn't fully understand. But, they made sense based on his life experience. Plus, the leaders had cars, girls and respect. Meeink wanted that – and an outlet for his frustration.

"It's hard to describe how good it felt to beat someone," he said. "It just felt so good to release that anger."

By 18, Meeink became a leader. He got tattoos displaying his ideology including a swastika on his neck. Then, the violence caught up with him. Meeink was sent to prison for assault and kidnapping. Looking to pass long days in the Illinois prison, Meeink met some African-American ball hockey players.

Meeink says, "You couldn't find anyone more racist than me." But, he loved the game and needed the escape. Through his skill, the other skinheads believed he was "representing" their colour. But, Meeink soon found unexpected commonality.

Meeink began speaking with the players after games. The topic always turned to girls. The skinheads were primarily lifers whose wives and girlfriends were gone. Like Meeink, the African-American players were serving shorter sentences. They too had girlfriends on the outside. After games, the egos broke down as they analyzed every word of love letters and anxiously awaited new ones.

Upon release, Meeink returned to Philadelphia. He met with old friends but found his belief system rocked by jail. He saw holes in his ideology and found himself disillusioned by the racist cause.

Confused, he turned back to hockey.

In his neighbourhood, the rundown rinks were a gathering place. With players dressed head-to-toe in gear, skin colour wasn't visible – only ability. He saw small guys show off. He saw big guys you normally wouldn't mess with unable to manoeuvre.

"These guys would step on the ice and crash in a minute," he said.

Thinking back to the prison love letters and ball hockey, Meeink saw his chance to break down egos and help others learn from his mistakes.

Starting in Philadelphia and now in Des Moines, Iowa, Meeink founded Harmony Through Hockey. The program teaches children teamwork, athleticism and tolerance.

Kids come from all races and backgrounds. Most have never played so they begin at the same level. They learn teamwork and improve together. Meeink gives them off-ice assignments like doing something nice for someone without saying anything and telling a teammate three things you like about them.

Using positive attitudes and camaraderie, Meeink eliminates what he felt as a child – hate. Through self-esteem and bonds with teammates from different backgrounds, the kids see the holes in hateful ideology sooner.

"They will all fall on their little butts but that knocks the ego right out," says Meeink.

That's a good thing. Falling is what he says offered salvation.

"You hear about some people giving their lives to hockey," he says. "Well for me, hockey owes me nothing and I owe it everything."

Discussion Questions:

1. What were the conditions that led Meeink to join a hate group? How did prison demonstrate the flaws in their arguments?
2. Why is hockey, or other sports, a good platform on which to teach tolerance? How can teaching positive attitudes, self-esteem and camaraderie eliminate hate?

***

Shining a light on Darfur, and elsewhere
July 20, 2009

There's not much new about the genocide in Darfur.

For six years now, the conflict has uprooted over two million people. The United Nations estimates about 300,000 have died while thousands of women have been raped.

The fact so little is changing makes the situation tragic. It's also what stifles news coverage.

Darfur isn't the only place where the "nothing new" status pushes reporting out of the mainstream. The Democratic Republic of Congo's 13-year conflict is rarely reported even though it's been named the deadliest since WWII. The Somali Civil War, ongoing since 1991, is today only covered in stories of pirate attacks off the country's coast.

There's little new. And, as media outlets compete with short attention spans and shorter budgets, dedicating coverage to "depressing" and expensive reporting of these regions is a luxury few can afford.

But Darfur does receive more headlines and political awareness than these other long-standing conflicts. One of the key reasons is Nicholas Kristof's reporting.

Since 2004, the *New York Times* reporter has travelled to the region many times. He's navigated roadblocks using frequent flyer cards pretending to be UN passes to report from razed villages. A Pulitzer Prize in 2006 made the public take notice. That included celebrities and policymakers.

Despite the fact little has changed, Kristof keeps risking his life by going back.

"I spent a lot of my career abroad," he says. "It made me attuned to the world. I came to think that news can add value by focusing on things that we're not paying enough attention to."

Around the world, journalists like Kristof put themselves in harm's way to cover stories no one else is talking about. There are also numerous publications committed to making space for their pieces. Each of them, journalist and publication alike, deserve praise.

Unfortunately, they are a dying breed.

Across the industry, advertising revenues are down and few readers pay for online content. Angryjournalist.com sells T-shirts stating, "Journalists get laid(off)." Kristof's newspaper is surviving by selling its assets and taking a $250 million loan with a 14 per cent interest rate.

Foreign bureaus are easy targets as newspapers make cuts to satisfy their budgets. Maintaining bureaus is incredibly expensive. Plus, the public is more easily wooed by cheaper-to-write stories involving celebrity gossip.

But losing the coverage is beneficial to no one.

"We went into journalism because we wanted to make a difference, not because we wanted to increase profit margins," said Kristof. "That desire to make a difference is why we have to make an effort to cover these stories."

Kristof spoke of one story involving a young woman in Darfur who had been raped. She hadn't told anyone in her village what happened because of the stigma involved. But, she insisted Kristof use her real name and picture in the newspaper.

"She said, 'This is the only way I can fight back,'" he explained.

To us, this story is not only a shining example of what journalism can do, but also why it is so essential. Kristof's byline carries weight. When it accompanies stories on Darfur, people get to know the conflict. That way, the public stays informed and the complex issue remains on the agenda.

And, most importantly, the woman gets a chance to fight back.

Despite belief that stories about Darfur and ongoing conflicts are disheartening, we think that's all a matter of perspective. If you look deeper, while the woman's story of rape and genocide is heart-wrenching, her courage and drive is anything but hopeless.

Certainly, the media has a lot of obstacles it must overcome. But cutting coverage of important issues from Darfur to Congo to Somalia any further is neither a solution nor an option.

Really, there's not much new about that.

Discussion Questions:
1. Why do media outlets often limit their coverage of ongoing conflict? Are these stories that you would like to hear more about? How could you encourage your newspaper to increase their reporting on certain issues?
2. Why did the woman who Kristof interviewed in Darfur say his reporting was the only way she could fight back? Is there a social issue that you would like to write about for your local newspaper?

✳✳✳

Dalai Lama sees Tibet's future in education
October 26, 2009

His Holiness the Dalai Lama has an incredible laugh. It's friendly, deeply genuine and often accompanied by two large grins – his and inevitably your own.

It was during a one-on-one interview with Craig that we heard this very laugh.

After the question, "What advice would you give your next reincarnated self?" the Dalai Lama chuckled and exclaimed, "I don't know!" He explained he had never been asked that question before.

The Dalai Lama is not only the Tibetan spiritual leader, he is believed to be a reincarnation of Chenrezig, the *bodhisattva* who embodies compassion. When the predecessor dies, he is thought to be reborn as a young boy. After a search by the other High Lamas, the new leader is confirmed.

But for Tenzin Gyatso, the fourteenth and current Dalai Lama, when his next life comes to being, passing on advice to him will be more complicated than with previous leaders. That's because the Chinese government has claimed exclusive rights to approve the selection of the reincarnation.

For 50 years, the monk has lived as a refugee. After the Chinese invasion of Tibet in 1949, the Dalai Lama (only then in his late-teens) travelled to Beijing for negotiations with Mao Zedong. But, after a failed national uprising, he was forced into exile in India in 1959.

"It's sad if you look at it from that angle," he says. "But if you look from another angle, in India, a free country, I had the opportunity of meeting with different people, learning through these meetings."

Seeing good is sometimes a hard perspective to take. But, there is certainly truth to his words.

For a half-century now, the Dalai Lama has travelled the world speaking on behalf of Tibet's autonomy while maintaining his culture and tradition from exile. While speaking out has actually put the institution of the Dalai Lama in jeopardy, it's also helped spread his message of compassion and empathy around the world.

It is truly a beautiful message. But, it's one that hasn't much improved the situation in Tibet or the stability to the Dalai Lama's future. Demographics are not working in his favour as the Chinese population increases within the region, further diluting the culture.

Tibet is no closer to independence than it was 50 years ago. A growing number of young people are expressing that change isn't happening quickly enough. That's why we asked what advice he had for the next generation.

"I don't think it's necessary for my advice," he replied. "Now, already last year there was a show, a crisis, in the entire Tibet area including four Chinese provinces where ethnic groups remain there. So, the peaceful demonstration took place, mainly those people who were involved in those demonstrations were young people. Afterward I heard there was a lot of suffering. Serious. Many killed, many disappeared, many tortured. And many imprisoned.

"But they all say the Tibet spirit became much, much stronger."

That spirit will be tested as the Dalai Lama ages. With Beijing's determination to approve his reincarnation, it seems the institution will soon end. That's why His Holiness asks his people to prepare through education.

"What I tell Tibet is education, modern education is very essential," he says. "We are carrying our struggle strictly through non-violence. So, in order to carry on a non-violent struggle effectively, education."

Through that education, he says, while the 600-year-old tradition might end, its teachings will always have significance.

"It is important to have full knowledge about what is the real Buddhist teaching, what is the real Buddhist. Then you will get some kind of conviction," he says. "It is something, not just ancient tradition. But also, in today's world, it is very much relevant."

Discussion Questions:

1. How has speaking out been both bad and good for the institution of the Dalai Lama?
2. How does the Dalai Lama hope education will keep the institution alive, even if there is no formal successor? What do you think China's insistence that their government pick the next Dalai Lama will do to the institution?

✽✽✽

Sustainability a lofty but attainable goal
December 14, 2009

Nothing about Ray Anderson's sombre pinstriped suit screamed mountaineer. Nonetheless, the 75-year-old is 60 per cent of the way up his personal Everest.

We recently saw the Atlanta-based businessman in Canada discussing his latest book, *Confessions of a Radical Industrialist.* It's a travel diary of sorts detailing his trek up Mount Sustainability and how he made a significant profit while doing so.

Mount Sustainability has a lofty, metaphorical peak – a zero carbon footprint for Interface, Anderson's carpet company. It first came to fame in the 2003 documentary, *The Corporation*.

Carpeting is one of many industries that are often overlooked in the environmental movement. When we think sustainability, we usually think cars, water bottles and light bulbs – not the soft fibres under our feet.

For 21 years, neither did Anderson.

After starting Interface in 1973, Anderson admits he gave the environment no serious thought. But in 1994 when customers started asking questions, Anderson began reading and was shocked by his findings.

"I was flummoxed, I wanted to throw up when I heard how much we were extracting from the earth," he says. "I resolved if there is going to be 1,000 or 10,000 generations of humans yet to come, our environmental impact needs to be zero."

That's when Anderson started his ascent.

"This was a big undertaking," he says. "We realized the mountain had seven faces. We needed to clear each face in order to clear the top."

The first face was to eliminate waste. Interface began redesigning its products and processes to reduce and simplify. Material waste was remanufactured into new resources. In doing this, Anderson estimates they cut waste by more than half, diverted 100 million pounds of material and saved $372 million.

"That's a huge cost saver and avoider," he says. "The progress we made on this face has paid for the mountain climb."

Next, by creating factories without smokestacks and effluent pipes, Interface reduced its emissions by 30 per cent as it moves steadily towards zero. That is being helped along by the mountain's third face – renewable energy. So far, Interface has converted seven of its facilities to operate on 100 per cent renewable energy like solar, wind and biomass.

Anderson then looked to change the linear "take-make-waste" process. For most companies, materials are extracted, made into products and discarded at the end of its lifecycle. Instead, Interface looked to make that process cyclical by recycling synthetics and keeping organics uncontaminated so they can be returned to nature.

That ensures at the end of a product's lifecycle, it doesn't become waste. Instead, it becomes a resource in making something new.

Interface continued up the mountain by reducing and moving towards resource-efficient transportation. By taking part in a number of voluntary emissions-offsetting programs, Interface has planted 87,000 trees since 1997. That's helped reduce the impact of 174 million business-related miles.

That brings Anderson to the sixth face – shifting mindsets. Anderson constantly campaigns his message. And, through a speaking bureau at Interface, many employees deliver sustainability-focused speeches around the world.

"We need to realize we don't live on an infinite earth," says Anderson. "We make a profit to exist. But, we must exist for some purpose."

With Interface striving to fully meet these goals by 2020, Anderson is working on summiting to the seventh face – one that stems directly from changing mindsets.

He explains there is a need to create an honest marketplace with new business models of sustainability. By proving to stakeholders that a business can be both profitable and sustainable, Anderson hopes others with follow, helping to redefine commerce by joining Interface on the peak.

Only then can we leave something for the next generation.

"We have to remember what we learned as children," says Anderson. "You can't squeeze the golden goose to death."

Discussion Questions:
1. Ray Anderson continued to make a profit when his business became more sustainable. How can you save money while being more environmentally-friendly in your day-to-day activities?
2. Think about your own career ambitions. What is important to you when it comes to choosing a place of work?

Teaching next generation to 'think higher, feel deeper'

February 7, 2010

Elie Wiesel says he is grateful. So much so that he constantly thanks everyone around him.

The waiter for their service. The taxi driver for the ride.

"There are no small things when it comes to gratitude," said the Holocaust survivor, Nobel Peace Prize winner and author of *Night* in a one-on-one interview with Craig. "Simply think if you or I can give a piece of bread to a hungry person, how grateful I am simply for being capable or adequate or wealthy enough to give that piece of bread."

This fits right into his mantra: "think higher and feel deeper."

The 81-year-old professor explained that thinking higher involves searching for meaning. It's not simply the act of giving bread. It's reflecting on what the gesture means by looking at it in relation to our social status and what we are grateful for. Feeling deeper involves feeling emotion from the very depths of our being.

"I want to sensitize my students. That is the real goal," he says. "And my listeners, when they hear me or they read me, they become more sensitive to another person's pain, another person's anguish, or to another person's joy."

Wiesel has dedicated his life to fighting indifference and intolerance. Through this personal mantra, he takes on the ultimate goal of connecting humanity. That, he hopes, will promote a more peaceful, more tolerant world.

"I have been a professor for so many years, which means I've taught thousands of young people. I can guarantee you that not one of them has ever chosen afterwards... the option of indifference," he says. "But, at the same time... morality does not play an important role in world affairs." He ponders how moral individuals become collective bystanders.

"It bothers me. It disturbs me. It pains me."

Wiesel describes himself as an idealist and a romantic. But, with politics often plagued by inaction, it's a position that's often emotionally painful to maintain.

"You hear about the economy, about strategy," he says. "But, not about morality."

That's why Wiesel places so much hope in the next generation.

Wiesel says today people are more in tune to the pain and suffering of their fellow man. In the 1930s, shortly before he entered Auschwitz as a 15-year-old, he points out only a handful of human rights organizations existed. Today, there are countless. And, although genocides existed prior to Wiesel's generation, today they are better documented and more widely taught. As a result, young people have developed a willingness to take action in order to prevent them from happening again.

"Rwanda, it remains a mark of shame on humanity's memory," he says. "Many of us had seen it coming, surely those in power. They could have prevented the massacre, the mass murder in Rwanda, but they didn't.

"So therefore the children today say, what the generation of our parents hasn't done, we are not allowing it to happen again."

Wiesel points to Darfur as an example. The crisis in this region spawned protests and calls for action on college and university campuses around the world. While he admits the problem hasn't yet been solved as hunger and human rights violations still persist, this mass mobilization challenged governments to take action.

"Our outrage has prevailed upon our leaders to do something more than say a few nice words," he says. "This generation really gives me hope. But, I am biased. I am a teacher."

Still, he adds, his view of youth doesn't mean that older generations can't do their part. If everyone can think higher and feel deeper, then we each can play a role in fighting indifference.

"What I learned, I learned that there is always a child in us and I am responsible not just for the children that I teach but also for the child still in me," he says. "I don't want to disappoint that child."

Discussion Questions:

1. What does Elie Wiesel's mantra "think higher, feel deeper" mean to you? In what ways can you follow this mantra in your own life?

2. How can passing on the stories of past suffering play a role in fighting indifference? Why is it important to be a witness?

Acknowledgements

In the past four years, we have been supported by many dedicated people whose collective efforts help to make Global Voices.

We are especially grateful to every person who has lent their expertise, their wisdom and their stories to this column. Behind each piece is an individual who eloquently shared their accounts of both happiness and hardship alike. We are constantly moved by their willingness to have their stories printed for others to read. Global Voices would not be possible without the openness, kindness and strength of these remarkable people.

Thank you to Sapna Goel, Chris Mallinos, Drew Davidson, TJ Arch and Henry Claflin for their dedication and patience throughout the writing process. Each of these remarkable individuals has spent hundreds of hours in research, interviews and writing. The Global Voices column, curriculums and school engagement program would not exist without their extraordinary passion to empowering the next generation to become passionate about global affairs. It has been a pleasure and honour to work with each of these individuals who we consider colleagues and friends.

Also to the Me to We Books team of Russ McLeod, Ryan Bolton, Marc Henry, Don Lane, Olga Kidisevic, Scott Lew, Laura Trethewey and Adam Long. The layout and design is the result of the design expertise of Frances Data. The illustrations accompanying each chapter would not be possible without the creative vision of Matthew Ng.

Me to We Books is grateful to the dedicated team at Douglas & McIntyre and Greystone Books. A special thank you to Scott McIntyre, Rob Sanders, Richard Nadeau, Susan Rana, Carra Simpson and the whole team. This book would not be possible without our friends and supporters at Participant Media, especially Jeff Skoll, Jim Berk, Bob Murphy, Jeffrey Ivers, Karen Frankel and Ricky Strauss.

Our thanks go out to David Aisenstat and the Keg Spirit

Foundation. Their continued dedication to supporting the education and development of young people is truly remarkable. Because of their commitment and generosity, this publication and the stories shared within it are being made available to thousands of students and classrooms across North America.

Global Voices would not appear in the *Toronto Star* and the *Vancouver Sun* each week without the contributions of a dedicated team. We would like to thank the *Toronto Star* including Chris Carter and Lorne Silver for their constant enthusiasm. At the *Vancouver Sun*, we are grateful for the commitment of Kevin Bent, Patricia Graham, Amanda Holland, Fazil Milhar and Harvey Enchin.

One of our favourite aspects of Global Voices is the educator resources that accompany the column each week. These resources are possible thanks to the Educators Financial Group, specifically Marianna Taggio, Sylvie Pelletier and the Committee for Community Care. We owe a very special debt of gratitude to Catherine McCauley for leading the charge on the educator resources for many years, and for constantly bringing creativity, vision and passion to each week's curriculum. From our own staff, we want to thank Amy Schlein for helping to launch this initiative as well as Corinne Impey and Heather Farragher for constantly being its champions. This compilation is accompanied by an educator resource guide, which is a result of the hard work of Rebecca McAllister.

Our gratitude goes out to all the school boards and educators who believe in the Global Voices program, especially Gerry Connelly, Chris Spence, Jeff Hainbuch, Allan Hux, Mark Lowry and the Toronto District School Board students, principals and teachers. We also remain thankful for the support of Greg Rogers, Mike Consul and the Toronto Catholic District School Board family. We have had the honour to work with educators in more than 3,500 schools across North America. We believe that teachers are the unsung heroes of our society.

This compilation directly ties into Free The Children's more than 15 years of work in the field of human rights and youth empowerment. We are especially grateful for the support of our board of directors, staff, volunteers and youth members.

Free The Children is blessed to have the tremendous vision and leadership of Dalal Al-Waheidi, who has become family. Me to We's activities have been built by the unwavering dedication and hard work of Renee Hodginkson. Thank you to the leadership team of Victor Li, Erin Blanding, Lloyd Hanoman, Shobha Sharma, Peter Ruhiu, Michelle Hambly, William Qi, Erin Barton-Chéry, Dan Kuzmicki, Lindsey Coulter, Sapna Goel, Allison Sandmeyer, Ashley Hilkewich, Scott Baker, Robin Wiszowaty, Marianne Woods, Kate Likely, Rann Sharma, Alex Apostol, Janice Sousa, Kim Plewes and Louise Kent.

Thanks to Roxanne Joyal for her years of partnership and support.

Love to our Mimi, who remains our biggest fan.

We would not be where we are today without the love and support of our parents, Fred and Theresa. Thanks for *everything*, Mom and Dad!

Index

Open your classroom to the world...

with the Global Voices Educators Resource Guide

Students are aware of the headlines and need the tools to understand the issues. Global Voices gives educators the opportunity to inspire students through issues-based activities and discussion.

The Global Voices Educators Resource Guide includes discussion points, questions and classroom activities aimed at sparking discussions, enhancing media literacy and developing critical thinking skills.

To get your classroom's copy, go to **www.metowe.com/books.**

About Free The Children

FREE THE CHILDREN
children helping children through education

Free The Children is the world's largest network of children helping children through education, with more than one million youth involved in its innovative education and development programs in 45 countries. Founded in 1995 by international child rights activist Craig Kielburger, Free The Children has a remarkable record of achievement, initiating community-based development projects around the world and inspiring young people to develop as socially conscious global citizens. Today, through the voices and actions of youth, Free The Children has built more than 650 schools in developing countries around the world, providing education to more than 55,000 students every day. Visit **www.freethechildren.com** to learn more.

213

About Me to We

ᙁ me to we

Me to We is a new kind of social enterprise for people who want to help change the world with their daily choices. Through our media, products and leadership experiences, we support Free The Children's work with youth creating global change. Every trip, T-shirt, song, book, speech, thought, smile and choice adds up to a lifestyle that's part of the worldwide movement of *we*.

Me to We offers choices that allow people to create ripples of positive change. What's more, through significant financial and in-kind donations, Me to We supports Free The Children's development work in marginalized communities worldwide. Visit **www.metowe.com** to find out more.

216

If you want to really experience another culture and truly see the world, take a Me to We trip.

Sure, you could lounge on yet another beach, surrounded by other stressed-out visitors seeing the usual tourist traps. But why not seek out a volunteer travel experience that radically changes your perspective, while positively transforming the lives of others?

Our staff live and work in the communities you'll visit, coordinating schoolbuilding and supporting development in participation with local communities. On a Me to We trip, you'll learn leadership skills, experience new cultures and forge truly meaningful connections.

Over 3,000 adventurous people of all ages have chosen to volunteer abroad with us. You'll do incredible things, like build schools and assist on clean water projects. You'll meet exuberant children excited at new possibilities for learning, and be immersed in local communities in ways never otherwise possible.

You'll get your hands dirty digging wells and laying foundations. But you'll love it. You'll come home with a sunburn—and the biggest smile you've ever had on your face. And best of all, you'll have memories that last a lifetime.

Visit **www.metowe.com/trips** to learn more.

Global Voices

Global Voices is a classroom-based program aimed at developing global citizens. This program gives educators the opportunity to inspire their students to change the world through issues-based activities and discussion.

Sign up for free, weekly activities delivered to your e-mail at **www.freethechildren.com**

Become a Junior Journalist

Young people are encouraged to share their perspectives by writing articles on social justice issues as part of the Junior Journalist team. Students who sign up are given the opportunity to enhance their writing skills by learning the fundamentals of reporting. Then, they get their stories published, along with Craig and Marc's column, each week.

Keep up-to-date with the latest:

 twitter.com/craigkielburger

 facebook.com/craigkielburger

 youtube.com/freethechildrenintl

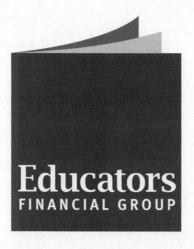

Educators
FINANCIAL GROUP

Global Voices is made possible by Educators Financial Group.

Thanks to their generous contributions, students have the opportunity to take part in meaningful discussions on current affairs. Educators Financial Group is supporting educators in classrooms by helping present this column and its curriculum to young people every week.

The World Needs Your Kid: Raising Children Who Care and Contribute
Craig and Marc Kielburger and Shelley Page

This unique guide to parenting is centred on a simple but profound philosophy that will encourage children to become global citizens. Drawing on life lessons from such remarkable individuals as Jane Goodall, Elie Wiesel and Archbishop Desmond Tutu, award-winning journalist Shelley Page and Marc and Craig Kielburger demonstrate how small actions make huge differences in the life of a child and can ultimately change the world.

Free the Children
Craig Kielburger

This is the story that launched a movement. *Free the Children* recounts 12-year-old Craig Kielburger's remarkable odyssey across South Asia, meeting some of the world's most disadvantaged children, exploring slums and sweatshops, fighting to rescue children from the chains of inhumane conditions.

My Maasai Life
Robin Wiszowaty

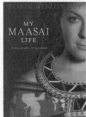

In her early '20s, Robin Wiszowaty left the ordinary world behind to join a traditional Maasai family. In the sweeping vistas and dusty footpaths of rural Kenya, she embraced a way of life unlike she'd ever known. With full-colour photographs from her adventures, Robin's heart-wrenching story will inspire you to question your own definitions of home, happiness and family.

Take Action! A Guide to Active Citizenship
Craig and Marc Kielburger

Want to begin changing the world? *Take Action!* is a vivid, hands-on guide to active citizenship packed with the tools young people need to make a difference. Accomplished human rights activists Marc and Craig Kielburger share valuable tips and advice from their experiences as founders of Free The Children and the Me to We movement. Ideal for grades 8–10, *Take Action!* shows that young people don't need to wait to be the leaders of tomorrow—this journey begins now.

Take More Action: How to Change the World
Craig and Marc Kielburger with Deepa Shankaran

Ready to take the next step? *Take More Action* is our advanced guide to global citizenship, empowering young people to be world-changers—around the world or in their own backyard.

Brilliantly illustrated and packed with powerful quotes, stories and resources, *Take More Action* includes invaluable material on character education, ethical leadership, effective activism and global citizenship. Ideal for Grades 10 and up, *Take More Action* paves the way for a lifetime of social action.

The Making of an Activist
Craig and Marc Kielburger with Lekha Singh

Warning: this book will change you. Full of vivid images and inspiring words, travelogues, poems and sparkling artwork, *The Making of an Activist* is more than just a scrapbook of Free The Children's remarkable evolution. It's a testament to living an engaged, active and compassionate life, painting an intimate portrait of powerful young activists. Explore the book. Catch the spark.

It Takes a Child
Craig Kielburger and Marisa Antonello; Illustrated by TurnStyle Imaging

It was an ordinary morning like any other. Twelve-year-old Craig Kielburger woke to his alarm clock and hurried downstairs to wolf down a bowl of cereal over the newspaper's comics before school. But what he discovered on the paper's front page would change his life—and eventually affect over a million young people worldwide.

It Takes a Child is a fun, vibrant look back at Craig's adventures throughout South Asia, learning about global poverty and child labour. This incredible story truly demonstrates you're never too young to change the world.

The Buy a Book, Give a Book promise ensures that for every Me to We book purchased, a notebook will be given to a child in a developing country.